LIFE IS FOR LIVING

By Theresa A. Morse

LIFE IS FOR LIVING

THE BEST I EVER TASTED

NEVER IN THE KITCHEN WHEN COMPANY ARRIVES

FUTURE A LA CARTE

LIFE IS FOR LIVING

Theresa A. Morse

Doubleday & Company, Inc., Garden City, New York

ISBN: 0-385-04477-1
Library of Congress Catalog Card Number 73–80735
Copyright © 1973 by Theresa A. Morse
All Rights Reserved
Printed in the United States of America

INTRODUCTION

In her book, Mrs. Morse, with a rare combination of compassion and firmness, accompanies a grief-stricken widow, whose feelings of numb hollowness have replaced those of one who had been a fulfilled wife. She arrives with her to the point where the widow can start being a forward-looking, affirmative person who is becoming a whole woman again.

Mrs. Morse's book falls naturally into three areas of dynamic exploration.

The first one describes, with painful lucidity, the never-ending sense of loss with its constant reminder of what has been and can never be again.

The second area moves into the chilling necessity of taking hold of the practical tasks of the management of one's widowed state.

The final area, all self-pity left behind, deals with the requirement of facing forward, of recognizing, as the title of the book announces, that life is for living; that there is still opportunity for enrichment for oneself and valuable contributions one can make to others.

Mrs. Morse is particularly helpful in the first section of the book in giving support to those who allow grief its passionate expression. No "stiff upper lip" for her! This is not the moment to put others ahead of oneself. That price, in the end, is unwholesome for all, she correctly insists. She makes clear, also, that death inevitably "leaves a trail of unfinished business." There is, of course, no longer an opportunity to make amends, to resolve abrasive differences. The finality, particularly as it relates to this emotional area, is a tormenting pressure. It causes relentless feelings of remorse and guilt, anger and resentment that seemingly now can never be resolved.

By far the largest portion of Mrs. Morse's book deals with the second area, the management of one's widowed life. Here she offers persuasive wisdom embodied in concrete examples that make one both laugh and think. Suppose you don't like your husband's lawyer. What then? In your bewildered state, should you talk to your children about finances? If not, to whom? You are very vulnerable. Who is likely to take advantage? If you hate living alone, should you team up with another widow, sharing your life and home? Should you consider inviting your bachelor brother in, or accept your married daughter's invitation to live with her? Mrs. Morse comes up with some unusually imaginative suggestions about these discomfiting problems.

And in her chapters on attitudes toward jobs and continuing education, you find a valuable inventory of ideas with concrete resource facts, particularly helpful to those women who are now faced with new financial necessities.

The final area, in which the spirit is at last accessible to fresh experience, is written with verve and humor, although the pitfalls present in the search for companionship with men and the need for sexual fulfillment are not glossed over.

It is clear that Mrs. Morse is in spontaneous touch with her own feelings. There is an arresting candor about her observations in relation to the widowed state. It should be of warm comfort to those women who are tormented by some murky feelings that they are convinced they ought not to have. But her candor is not the sort of honesty, so often present in self-appointed advisers to widows, that is, in reality, a cover for small-mindedness, or a thin disguise for cruelty. There is no "blabbing the truth" in the name of forthrightness. Mrs. Morse shows a generosity of spirit toward herself and all the others encompassed in her discussion. It is a loving example to us all.

Ruth Pilpel Brickner, M.D.

FOREWORD

This is not a sociological study—it is a human document based on my own experience, conversations with friends, neighbors, and strangers across the country, as well as interviews with doctors, lawyers, and heads of such helpful organizations as the Widow to Widow Program in Boston (sponsored by the Laboratory of Community Psychiatry, Department of Psychiatry, Harvard Medical School) and the Widows Consultation Service in New York City.

This book was conceived in Mexico City when Carolyn Sammet and I compared experiences as we discussed the dangers and pitfalls inherent in returning to society as a widow. That conversation was followed by many others, and my first thanks go to her for help and inspiration.

Next Tom Scott and Robert Somerlott, heads of the Writers' Workshop in the Instituto Allende at the University of Guanajuato, stiffened my backbone, bullied me into slavery, cheered, and encouraged.

Third, my brother-in-law, Manuel D. Goldman, an attorney in Rochester, New York, provided not only loving support and interest, but checked and counterchecked all legal information.

AND my daughter, Carol Morse Feiner, who helped all the way.

Many others lent a helping hand. At no time did I ask anyone for an interview (from busy doctors to newly bereaved women) and meet with a refusal. Letters were often answered with telephone calls, introductions were arranged wherever I went, government offices were immensely helpful as were libraries—especially The Rundel Library in Rochester, New York, and the Vineyard Haven Library on Martha's Vineyard.

The following is an alphabetical list of those benefactors to whom I am most indebted: Ms. Ruth D. Abrams, research social worker; Ms. Margaret H. Baum; Ms. Elizabeth R. Bernkopf; Ms. Bess Dana, Associate Professor, Department of Community Medicine, Mount Sinai School of Medicine; Jim Egleson, co-author of *Parents Without Partners;* Ms. Jane A. Goldman; Dr. Russell S. Hoxsie; Ms. Elizabeth Duncan Koontz, Director of Women's Bureau, U. S. Department of Labor; Ms. Elizabeth R. Leydon; Ms. Dorothy Marks; Dr. Milton Mazer; Ms. Virginia Mazer; Ms. Eulalie M. Regan, Head Librarian, Vineyard Haven Library; Dr. Phyllis Silverman, Harvard Medical School; Ms. Margaret G. Van Raalte; George B. Williams, National Director, Parents Without Partners, Inc.; and John A. Willoughby.

CONTENTS

LIFE IS FOR LIVING

Chapter 1

YOUR IDENTITY CRISIS

It was a great day although there had been no warning, nothing to alert you that morning when you awoke to the same old sodden depression, that today would be different. Different because, for perhaps the first time since suffering the nightmare shock that splintered your life, you have been carried away by something entirely outside yourself.

Perhaps the miracle occurred on the way to market or en route to your job. No matter—it happened. Suddenly the sky is a dazzling blue, gentle breezes (or even icy winds) bring a feeling of well-being and, without thinking, you become absorbed in the antics of two small boys. While their Spock-oriented mothers patiently reason with them they happily shove each other into the nearest grubby mud-puddle. The sound of your laughter—rusty from disuse, but still laughter—fills your ears. For a few seconds you are engrossed, unaware of yourself, and this hasn't happened in weeks, maybe months. Your step quickens; you stand straighter; people, traffic, shop windows, food stalls swim into focus. You are on the threshold of a long, slow convalescence, but you are on the way back.

We, who have lost our husbands, have lost a part of ourselves. He, whom we loved the most, our best companion, audience, and admirer, the one who egged us on to achieve more than we ever believed possible and who, in turn, expected the same from us, has vanished from our lives. Vanished, leaving behind a vast, hollow emptiness with which we are unable to deal. Through the numbness, the agony, penetrate such searing questions as What will become of me? What am I going to do? How can I live alone?

There are no immediate answers to these painful questions but, for the time being, they can be shoved aside because at the moment of tragedy and for some time afterward, you are seldom alone. Children, family, and friends spell each other in an effort to comfort and distract you. But in your head (which doesn't seem to be functioning properly—even the newspaper doesn't make sense), you are deeply aware that the fearful day when you must face your painful reality is drawing closer and closer.

Echoes from conversations swirl and eddy about your head.

"Isn't she marvelous?"

"You'd expect her to be brave, wouldn't you?"

"What strength . . . what character. . . ."

The new You, the zombie You, hears, but very little registers. Temporarily you are insulated by grief, encased in misery, and only dimly aware of what is going on around you. Vague, remote, often forgetful, you will go through familiar motions without coming to terms either with yourself or your surroundings. Perhaps you will talk incessantly about your husband, unwittingly exaggerating his virtues, idealizing this man who, in real life, undoubtedly was heir to human frailties like the rest of us. Perhaps you are unable to talk about him at all as you run the gamut of fear, frustration, and finally anger. You will spin from depression to fury. Why did this have to happen to me? Why *me*? Abandoned, deserted . . . nothing will shake your belief that your situation is different from all others, your suffering more painful, your grief more acute.

Through all this you are Exhibit A, the star of the show, the one about whom all thought and action center, even though you may be unaware of this unwelcome limelight. For the time being you are in limbo, encased in a tight cocoon of misery and confusion. Whether death struck suddenly or gave warning, grief will overwhelm you. No matter how long a marriage you had, if it was happy, it ended too soon. If only you could have had five, ten, twenty years more together. No matter what his age, he was too young, he had too many unfulfilled hopes and plans. Even when death brings an end to incurable illness and suffering, there is only cold comfort, accompanied by the deep-seated conviction that a cure might have been, must have been, just around the corner. For perhaps the first time in your life you will read the obituaries, and whenever you find the name of someone younger than your husband, you will know a shameful grain of comfort.

Out of the chaos of ringing telephone and door bells, people come and go. The ones that mean the most will be the children who loved their father; the special sister, sensitive and protective; the brother-in-law who quietly takes charge, infusing strength and order. Or the close friend who, having been through this grief, with understanding and tact will act as a buffer between you and the hordes around you.

You will need a buffer for, inevitably, you will be exposed to some who thrive on misfortune. These are the sympathizers who will tear you apart with cloying pity. Nothing they say will be right. That maddening refrain, "time is a great healer," will beat on your ears over and over again. True or false, you don't believe it, don't want to hear about it. Equally infuriating is the cliché, "You must have such happy memories." Who needs memories? Or the syrupy bromide, "Lucky you to have had twenty-thirty-forty (whatever) years together." You don't feel the least bit lucky. Just the opposite.

How do *they* know so much? They don't. What makes them so omniscient? They're not. So fight back by being temperamental. This is the one time in your life when you can do as you please, so let your instinct for self-preservation protect you. See only those people whom you love and who bring comfort.

Mail is another pitfall into which you will unwittingly stumble. It would seem that news of your loss has spread across the country and that everyone who knew you and/ or your husband feels impelled to write.

Some of these letters will be godsends—warm, comforting words telling you what you most want to hear from people you cherish. Often they will urge you not to bother answering—they are writing only because they want you to know how much they love you and share your grief. The telegram from a dear friend, thousands of miles away, saying, "I am holding your hand," is like a close embrace that you will keep in your heart forever. Equally comforting is the letter from a friend of your childhood:

"I was shocked to learn of your husband's death and send you my deep sympathy. Only lately do I begin to grasp something of what it means to lose one's most intimate companion. It means nothing less than building a new life with strength one has acquired from the old. What one learns in the loss of those closest is that there is a living legacy, a still-developing personality, profoundly part of one's own. One chapter ends, to be sure, but the next is at once based on it and has its own important development."

Others write glowingly of your husband—his charm, humor, intelligence, charisma . . . all of which underscores your loss but, at the same time, is deeply comforting. Some of the letters will come from people whom you have never known—childhood friends of your husband, former employees, business acquaintances, members of organizations to which he belonged. Their special brand of warmth and appreciation fills you with pride and gratitude.

Offsetting these letters come the ones from well-meaning fools. They will tell you that they understand your agony only too well because they, too, have suffered the same irreparable loss. You don't for a minute believe it. What's more, you don't want to hear about it. But the bulk of the mail will contain very short notes—brief, meaningless messages or commercial cards for the bereaved. Let your priority visitors assist in acknowledging them. They've been longing to help, and here is something they can do.

At first every day will bring problems interlaced with a good deal of unsolicited advice that, for the most part, will fall on deaf ears. Everything is a problem—sleep, food, clothes, mail, telephone calls, flowers, messages, and, too often, family.

The people closest to your grief—sons, daughters, in-laws—are suffering shock and loss of their own. "Knock her out" they implore your doctor at the time of death, in an effort to spare you and themselves as well. Temporarily this may be all right—but the doctors to whom I have spoken do not seem to think so. They agree that it helps immensely to give vent to the emotion of grief. To cry, to talk, to pace up and down, mitigates pain. An emotion expressed is a release of tension. The price for the so-called "stiff upper lip" can be devastatingly high at a later date. It helps when family say, "let it out, this must be dreadful for you, cry if you feel like it," thus furnishing proof that they understand. Conversely, you are defeated, turned off, by such words as, "don't cry, it's so bad for you. If you keep this up, you'll make yourself sick. . . ."

Those first days and nights are comparable to a time of acute illness. Your reflexes will be slow, your attention span brief, as your mind darts from the past to the present to the frightening future.

Daytimes are bad enough, but the nights are fierce. Guilt feelings, real or fancied, run rampant through your head. "If only I'd insisted on his seeing a doctor sooner." "Why didn't I go with him on that strenuous business trip?" "Why did I let him gain so much weight?" This exercise in futility is inevitable, but make it as short-lived as you possibly can. You weren't supposed to be your husband's keeper, nor he yours. He didn't have to smoke two packs of cigarettes a day, forget his pills half the time, insist on shoveling snow, drink too much at cocktail parties, or whatever. Were the situation reversed, he'd probably be beating himself up just as foolishly in your behalf.

The long, slow hours of the night can play fearsome tricks with your thinking. Lonely, unhappy—what is there left to live for in the bleak future that stretches ahead? During those black hours you will be assaulted by memories and battered by regrets and guilt feelings that are damaging and destructive. You will dredge up subtle torturous questions. Did you hold each other back, did you prevent him from reaching his full potential, was his illness so dreadful that you wished him to die and now suffer unbearable guilt because it has happened. Did you ever let him know, during that long, horrible illness, how much you loved him, how much your marriage meant to you. Were you so brave that he never saw you cry, although that might have comforted him as proof of how much you cared.

Guilt feelings are tricky: They sneak up on you, catch you unawares. Why did I make such a fuss whenever he suggested inviting the boss and his wife for dinner? Why did I loathe fishing when it meant so much to him? Why . . . why . . . why? Small episodes get blown up into outsized nightmares. Mrs. Curtis, happily married for over forty years to a man who never quite believed his luck in having her for his wife, suffered agonizing remorse because she had prevented her husband from opening a jar of homemade strawberry jam (reserved for dinner parties) at what turned out to be his last breakfast. One can only wonder what deeper guilt feeling this trivial incident triggered.

Don't worry about guilt feelings. Real or fancied, big or little, new or old, you are going to be plagued by them. *Everyone* is. The so-called "perfect marriage" is a myth. All of us humans, male or female, are endowed to a greater or lesser degree with temperament, hostility, aggressiveness, intolerance, as well as some of the more appealing qualities. We make mistakes, get overtired, lose our tempers, behave badly. Death has the power to distort the smallest incident. Inevitably it leaves a trail of unfinished business—regrets over old arguments that now can never be resolved. Why was the last thing I said unpleasant? Why didn't I say that I was sorry sooner?

Why him? Why did he have to die? Why not me? Why should I be alive when he is dead? Offsetting such guilt comes rage at his desertion, senseless anger that he didn't keep his affairs in better order, that his Will can't be found, or that he died on some dangerous junket against which you had warned him.

Claire S. could not dissuade her somewhat elderly husband from going off on a hunting trip "with the boys." When he left she angrily refused to either kiss him or say goodbye. On the trip he suffered a massive heart attack and died before reaching home. It was years before she forgave herself.

If you have lost your husband in a marriage that was intact—whether that marriage was good, relatively good, or less than good—the trauma of death will have a shattering impact, and you will know a temporary sense of numbness and amputation. Even if your marriage was a tumultuous one, it won't make the loss any easier to bear. The battles may have been an important, meaningful part of your life. Margaret J. fought her husband through thirty turbulent years. Everyone expected her adjustment to be quick and relatively easy. Instead she lapsed into a profound, long-lasting depression.

Depression, short-lived or interminable, is part of the syndrome of grief. Don't wait until your need for help is overwhelming. Instead, seek professional advice as fast as you can. Even if you seem to be getting along beautifully, making a fine adjustment—get some help. Yours may be a delayed reaction, which can be just as painful and troublesome as an immediate one. Find a Ph.D. in marriage counseling, a clinical psychologist, a psychiatric social worker, a psychiatrist, or a psychoanalyst—depending on where you are and who is available. You will need to ventilate this pain to a professional who will know how to deal with a reality, reactive depression. He can help you over some very rough spots, help you to regain your perspective and find yourself. For yours is presumably a normal grief reaction, not a serious neurotic problem, and the authoritative knowledge that others suffer the identical feelings of guilt and remorse, of rage and resentment, can speed your recovery. This cannot be achieved until feelings of guilt and anger are resolved.

The incidence of depression is high during the first six months following the death of a spouse. It is a widespread belief in the medical profession today that if every widow and widower could consult one of the professionals for as few as six or seven visits, such visits might prevent depression altogether.

Friends and family are not qualified to help. No matter how willing and eager they may be, they can only advise within the framework of their own limited experience. And hangups. They, too, are involved in your grief. As a matter of fact, death can be traumatic for an entire community. Let a member die of a heart attack and local doctors are besieged by patients suffering from "indigestion" and/or "chest pains" or coming in to ask for a physical when none was due. One doctor sheepishly admitted that, on the heels of two sudden deaths on the same day, he, himself, had undergone a "physical."

During the first difficult nights alone, sleep—elusive, longed-for sleep—is fitful at best, and the interminable hours of the night can terrify to the point of panic. This is where your family doctor comes in. He knows you through and through and, unless there is some valid reason against it, will make sure that for as long as you need help, you will sleep deeply and well.

Do what *he* recommends and don't listen to anyone else on the subject of medicine. Everyone seems to have a pet panacea and/or sleeping pills that they are willing and eager to share. "If you're feeling jittery, try these." "Here's something to calm you down." "These will make you sleep like a baby," they will say, and you will be swamped by an avalanche of red, yellow, and blue pills. Maybe yes, maybe no. "One man's meat . . ." and you are in no condition to be a guinea pig. Only your doctor knows what is best for you. He also knows what he's doing, so give him *all* of your medical business.

Start fresh. Toss out the prescription medicine in the cabinet that belonged to your husband. What helped him may be bad for you. Make an appointment for a physical examination as soon as possible. Grief and shock can trigger anything from ulcers to shingles, from fatigue to starvation, but your doctor can anticipate trouble and, in some cases, prevent it. You can help by not getting over-tired—an ever-present hazard as you struggle to deal with people, decisions, and responsibilities that never before were yours.

Dispose of your husband's clothes and other belongings as fast as you can—they will be constant, painful reminders of your grief. Perhaps he remembered sons, sons-in-law, grandsons, or brothers with keepsakes in his Will. If not, ask the man in the family closest to you to divide the gifts fairly. Clothes can be sent to any number of needy organizations.

Evelyn M. hit on a unique method of solving this problem. After the men in her family had chosen what they wanted, the remainder of her husband's belongings and clothes were placed in a guest room. She then invited all the local young men, who had served them in any way, to come and help themselves. Each was given a tote bag and told to go upstairs alone and take what he chose. They came by invitation at different hours—war veterans, delivery boys, painters, young working men with families, hippies. Eventually the little that was left was delivered to the local Thrift Shop.

Not only the nights but the days, too, can be fiendish, although, at first, there are usually people around to distract you. Still, they are not always on hand and, at times, driven by loneliness and fear, you will cast about frantically for relief. You look longingly at the liquor cabinet and realize, for perhaps the first time in your life, how easy it would be to find oblivion there. Perhaps you experiment; perhaps, deep within, you know that drinking offers no solution. The oblivion will be short-lived, the aftermath punishing. Drinks are good only for festive occasions—no magic release from sorrow is contained in those tempting bottles. Only unconsciousness, followed by depression and guilt.

These battles must be fought, and the going is rough. Your shattered, fragmented self is not equipped to fight, not ready to take action of any kind. No matter what your age, nor how many years of marriage you have experienced, the chances are that, sooner or later, you will fall apart. But, unlike Humpty Dumpty, it will be possible to put you together again.

Chapter 2

BEGINNING TO FIND YOURSELF

Gradually, a few at a time, friends and family who have
been standing by, protecting and caring for you, return
to their own lives and commitments. For a while they continue to be sensitively aware of you, especially if you are
living alone. Invitations to meals pour in, raising questions
in your mind that had never before occurred. Do they
really want you by yourself, or are they just sorry for you?
Can you bear seeing Joe carefully mixing Marge's special
martini, or watch Tom give Janet a hand at clearing the
table? In your home there no longer is the happy sound
of a man moving things about, checking the bar, filling
the ice bucket, surprising you by setting the table. It
takes time, lots of time, to get used to seeing this in other
homes without pain. Besides, you are still extremely vulnerable, and the unexpected appearance of an old friend,
a nostalgic song, or a sentence beginning, "Remember the
fun we used to have when we . . ." can reduce you to
tears.

Now friends will urge you to come to their dinner

parties: "It will do you good, take you out of yourself."
In a moment of desperation you may accept such an invitation, arguing with your reluctant self that something
is better than nothing and the party might furnish a
longed-for distraction. Don't be either surprised or em-
barrassed if, at the very last minute, you find yourself
backing out. It simply means that you are trying to tackle
a difficult situation too soon.

Go slowly. A gala party, before you are ready, can backfire and mow you down. Suddenly these good friends,
enjoying themselves, drinking, eating, behaving as though
it doesn't matter that your husband is dead, are fiends,
monsters. The intensity of your anger can cause you,
without warning, to dissolve in tears, run from the party,
do any number of things guaranteed to make a shambles
of yourself and those around you.

So, for a while, as with any convalescence, don't push
yourself too hard. A fever chart rises and falls; so will
your spirits. Recover slowly, gain a little at a time, go
where you can be comfortably yourself: to the homes of
married children, close relatives, or good friends. Anything else can be a strain on both you and your hosts.

But if you aren't going to accept dinner invitations,
at least not many, what are you going to do about food?
Daytime meals are a cinch. Breakfast is a small, relatively
unimportant meal to most of us, and we are accustomed
to grabbing a sandwich by ourselves for lunch. Besides,
people are still bringing over gallons of homemade chicken
soup (you'd like to know that you'll never see another drop
as long as you live), casseroles of all kinds, and delicious
little cookies because you have been refusing their invitations and they want to look out for you. And look *at*

you—make no mistake about that. They want to see for themselves how you are bearing up, how you are dealing with tragedy. Are you fat or thin, pretty or ugly, depressed or valiantly playing a role? As a matter of fact, peculiar changes often do take place. Fat ladies become slim; sloppy housekeepers become paragons of neatness; and gals indifferent to clothes become fashion plates. Sometimes this is accidental—if you lose interest in eating, inevitably you lose weight. Sometimes it is unconscious reform. Did he always admire chic, slim ladies—something you never were? No matter what, you will need protection from this morbid curiosity.

Dinner: There's the rub! Dusk, cocktail time, and dinner unleash loneliness and terror. No key turns in the lock, no voice sings out, "I'm home!" You, who have spent a good part of a lifetime preparing the food he most enjoys, timing your meal so that you can be free the instant your husband reaches home, now can find no reason, no sense to cooking. For yourself alone the barest minimum will do, whatever you can find in the refrigerator, and you might as well eat it in the kitchen.

Here's where you start getting tough with yourself. If you are not gainfully employed and can find a volunteer job beginning in the late afternoon, grab it. Nobody wants to work at that hour, so it shouldn't be difficult. Your local hospital can surely use you; so can other organizations that need telephones manned, envelopes stuffed and sealed, or a receptionist on duty at that unpopular hour.

Betsy G., a beautiful, talented artist very much in love with her husband, lost him immediately after their fourth and youngest child entered college.

"I could handle daytimes," she said, "but the early evenings when Arthur was due home were unbearable until I discovered Madame Carpentier's advertisement in our local paper."

Madame Carpentier was offering tea and French conversation every weekday afternoon from four-thirty to six-thirty for the astonishing sum of twenty dollars a month. Betsy joined the group and found delightful companionship as well as a splendid opportunity to improve her French. It turned out that this was Madame Carpentier's way of coping with the exact same problem. By the time Betsy returned home, the worst part of the late afternoon and early evening had been bypassed.

Dinner! No matter how simple, force yourself to prepare a tempting meal. Maybe it will be only a lamb chop, baked potato, and mixed green salad. The very act of preparing this food will keep you busy and tide you over a bad hour. Use good china, take the trouble to make the meal look as appetizing and attractive as possible. Serve it on a tray in some unfamiliar place—such as your bedroom with television turned on to the news (bless those male voices) or to some diverting program. You will be astonished one night to discover that the ringing telephone, coming in the middle of your dinner and the program, is an annoying interruption rather than a welcome signal that someone wants to talk to you. Besides, when you are ready to invite guests for dinner, you will still be comfortably at ease in the kitchen instead of timid and out-of-practice.

Lurking in the background waiting to pounce is the problem of finances. Perhaps you've never handled money, perhaps this was your husband's department—something he enjoyed doing while you were absorbed in children, home, and community projects. All of us know husbands who never quite believe their wives capable of dealing with money, or feel their own masculinity threatened unless they control the purse strings. Even if you did know something about his affairs, circumstances are entirely different now. You are in complete charge and at a time when you are both shattered and confused.

In your muddled head, income will have ceased entirely, capital will be tied up for many months in sluggish legal procedure (besides, if there are children, shouldn't the capital be kept intact for them?) and a variety of fees and disbursements will hang frighteningly over your head. No matter how large your husband's income may have been, nor how splendid your savings, nor how sufficient his life insurance, you may still feel overwhelmed by uncertainty and insecurity.

So, for perhaps the first time in your life, you very possibly will be afraid to spend an unnecessary cent. To your protesting family you keep insisting, "I must be very careful until I know exactly where I stand." Your children argue, remind you that they, themselves, have plenty and that, above all else, they want you to be comfortable. You don't listen, don't hear. Perhaps "How will I get along financially?" is just another way of saying to oneself, "How will I get along without him?"

Conversely, and only occasionally, we see the woman who, under these same circumstances, promptly goes off on a buying binge. We know her husband to have been both generous and beloved, yet, at breakneck speed, she buys expensive clothes, jewelry, a new car, furs, and all else that catches her eye. In exactly the way an unloved child eats her way to obesity in her futile search for love, so does this recently bereaved wife seek futile consolation for her loss.

Oddly enough, this new, careful, economical You can turn into a prize victim overnight. For this is the time when the men in your life, some of them at any rate, will spring to your financial rescue. Depending on who and what they are, they will come forward with some amazing offers. They have inside information on a stock that's sure to double in value in six months and they'd like to see you get in on the ground floor. Or, while they don't, as a rule, offer stock to outsiders, still, if you'd like to invest a few thousand in their business, they'll let you in. The business is in great shape and doing better every year. The husband of your best friend hints mysteriously that he's on to a very good thing and is willing to include some of your capital with his own.

Very tempting! How lovely to dump your financial burdens on those strong, helpful shoulders. How comforting to sit back and let others take care of you. What an expensive mistake it can prove to be.

Helen S., who, before the death of her husband, had never dealt with money or finances beyond her housekeeping allowance, found herself besieged with propositions as to how she should invest her husband's life insurance. Before she had committed herself, a close friend of her husband's came to see her.

"Helen," he said, "I imagine a lot of people are giving you financial advice and putting pressure on you to invest your money. I'd like to add my two cents' worth. *Don't listen to anyone!!* What *you* need is a team of experts to look after you."

"I've always had a wonderful team of experts," she said. "My husband, my minister, and my obstetrician."

"You need a second team now," he said gently. "A lawyer, an accountant, and an investment counselor."

All of us need some or all of that second team. We cannot afford to gamble, and certainly we cannot afford to lose. It is a truism in the legal profession that the vast majority of widows lose a substantial part of an uncontrolled bequest within seven years.

Don't talk about your affairs. In the first spasm of shock and grief, it's a great temptation to pour confidences into the ear of the nearest listener, to tell too much about your emotions, your erstwhile private relationship with your husband, your finances, and all else churning inside you. You will never regret what you haven't divulged and, once spoken, you cannot take it back. Everyone is curious, especially curious about Wills, the size of an estate, the way it is bequeathed. Don't satisfy that curiosity.

A few months after the death of Dorothy B.'s husband, a good friend said to her, "I worry about you—I do hope you're all right financially. If anything happened to my Russell, I doubt if I'd have enough to live on. How much does one actually need? What are you getting along on?"

Dorothy, recognizing unadulterated curiosity when she met it head on, parried with, "How much do you think you'd need?" and during the ensuing conversation made it extremely clear that the original questions were going unanswered.

Instead of talking impulsively about your affairs, seek professional advice, and that means finding a lawyer who is right for you. He is essential to your peace of mind and welfare. The probating of a Will and the administering of an estate require the services of an experienced lawyer. If you cannot relate to your husband's lawyer, if he doesn't inspire your confidence and, besides, you never liked him much anyway—no matter how much your husband admired and respected him—there is no disloyalty in finding someone else to work for you. You must have a lawyer with whom you can comfortably and frankly communicate.

Anything less can spell disaster. Between you and your lawyer should exist a doctor-patient relationship. By law he may not divulge your affairs to anyone, nor repeat any conversation he may have with you. Not even in a court of law is this permitted. Deal with him on a professional basis, which means consulting him only in his office and paying a fair fee for the privilege. Doctors and lawyers are sitting ducks for patients and clients who tackle them at social gatherings, on the street, and dozens of other places for a little free advice.

Your lawyer will help chart a financial course for you, see to it that you receive funds immediately from the estate, if necessary, and will help you to take a realistic inventory of your assets.

If you don't already know how, learn to balance your checkbook. It's an absolute must and, at the same time, learn to read your bank statements and understand the abbreviations on them. Make friends with stocks, bonds, savings accounts, investments—whatever may be included in your husband's estate. Know what you are doing— what you *can* do. You are now in charge, and wise and careful handling of money can make a tremendous difference to your life style and peace of mind. Once we understand something—even if it's bad news—we can handle it. As Franklin Roosevelt said, "The only thing we have to fear is fear itself."

A splendid booklet, well worth reading, is entitled *Money in Your Life*, and you can obtain a copy, at no charge, by writing to:

> Women's Division
> Institute of Life Insurance
> 277 Park Avenue
> New York, N.Y. 10017

Its Foreword states, "As a woman on your own, you may be single, widowed, separated, or divorced. You may be starting on your first job, well along in a career, or not working at all. Whatever your status, you are constantly making and carrying out decisions about the money in your life. The following pages present basic information to help you do so."

This booklet is designed not only to help you find the answers to your questions about money, but also provides space for recording your facts and figures, thus providing a convenient record all in one place.

The mechanics of probating a Will depend on the facts of each individual family situation. No one can generalize on this point. It is an involved, slow process, calling for patience on your part. For a while, at least, it will seem as though your lawyer is accomplishing nothing. After all, when you need a dentist, he's there and does the necessary work. All that your lawyer seems to do is take copious notes, then vanish. But from that point on he can't go any faster than the law allows, no matter how impatient you may be to "get things settled." This is one of many reasons why you must have confidence in him.

Reminder note! Once you have chosen your lawyer, get busy on your own Will. This can be a dangerous omission and cause endless complications for your heirs. Remember everyone you possibly can, and dispose fairly of family heirlooms, jewelry, and other treasures. Keep in mind that feelings are easily hurt, that everyone knows that your daughter is your favorite, and that your pitifully insecure daughter-in-law needs proof that you love her and thought of her. Don't leave anyone out because of a grudge. Wills can pull families together or tear them apart.

Perhaps you and your husband were unable to accumulate savings. Perhaps your investments were all in the future—banked in the education and training of your children. Perhaps there wasn't time for him to get ahead. Suggestions for solving job problems can be found in Chapter 6. But no matter how small the estate, you, too, will need help. Every woman, upon the death of her husband, is faced with some legal problem because, in our present society, everyone has an economic stake of one kind or another.

To what is your husband entitled from his firm, his union, his government? Benefits differ from company to company: insurance, pensions (union or company), severance death benefits. Your lawyer will be able to secure the maximum to which you are entitled in all areas. That includes Social Security and, if your husband served in the armed forces, veterans' benefits. Should there be an insurance policy in the estate, he can advise you as to

the respective merits of taking this money in one lump
sum or on the installment plan.

In any event, discuss your situation frankly with him
and ask, in advance, what his fee for handling your affairs
will be. If it is more than you feel that you can afford, ask
the trust officer at your bank for advice. This kind of as-
sistance differs from state to state; perhaps you will turn
to the Legal Aid Society or even to an officer of your
local bar association. There are also government agencies
designed to help, and your bank can point the way.

Don't discuss finances with your grown-up children if
you can possibly avoid doing so. For all these years you
and your husband have managed your affairs without
benefit of help or advice from your children. Continue
to do so. Feel free to do what is important and meaningful for you. Perhaps some purchase or trip will seem un-
necessarily extravagant to your son, but it may be extremely important for you. You must do what you, and
you alone, think best.

A well-known joke in my hometown, and one not far
from the truth, concerned Mrs. A., an attractive, middle-
aged widow with a splendid income. It was claimed that
she would not buy so much as a toothbrush without asking her son's permission, and that he always said, "No."
Mrs. D., on the other hand, carefully economized throughout the last twenty years of her life, spending the absolute minimum in order to keep her large capital intact
for her children. When she died, she left her two extremely successful sons a fortune but she, herself, had no
fun, no trips, no luxuries of any kind. Capital is not sacred,
not intended to be remote, untouchable. Use it sensibly
to help make a better life for yourself. It is rough re-

building a life. It helps immensely if one can afford some fun and comfort along the way.

Decisions, decisions, decisions! For a while you will passively struggle to get through one day at a time, side-stepping whatever doesn't require immediate attention. But one tormenting question in particular will spring at you whenever you are off-guard during any given day or night. Finally you can think of nothing else and are forced to face the major problem of where you should spend the remaining years of your life.

Assuming that your children are grown, whether you are in your forties, fifties, or sixties, you will want to make an immediate change. How can you go on living in your present house or apartment, so spacious and comfortable for two, so impossibly big for one? Filled to overflowing with mementos of your life together. Your eye travels slowly from the Crome landscape, found in a tiny water-front shop in San Francisco, to the cobbler's bench, purchased at an outdoor auction in Connecticut (where you sat together in the blazing sunshine, briskly bidding while eating a picnic lunch), to the lovely brass candlesticks bought one Saturday morning in a Mexican flea market. Now each is a separate stab of pain, and you will cast about frantically for an escape hatch.

One is dangerously close at hand. Sell the house, dispose of the furnishings, and start over again in a smaller place with different belongings. Let the children take what they want, then sell the rest.

Don't do it! Not any of it. At least not until you have waited at least a year. Perhaps you were right in the first place. Perhaps, for many reasons, a complete change of locale and furnishings is indeed the best solution for you.

But you must be absolutely certain. It is far more likely that, in time, your present home will become a warm refuge, and the furnishings will be happy reminders that you will cherish. In any case, the convalescing You is not qualified to make far-reaching, long-lasting decisions. You are not ready nor equipped to change your life style, and you dare not dispose of the accumulated treasures of decades without risking unending regrets. So, assuming that the choice is yours, stay where you are for the time being.

If, on the other hand, maintaining the home that you and your husband shared is now financially beyond you, then carefully assess the possibilities before deciding where to live. Obviously, if you are tied down to your present community by a job, children, or both, you are limited as to what you can do.

Assuming that you are free to choose, move carefully. Some women elect to return to their hometowns, where family and friends are still living. Sometimes this works, sometimes it doesn't. Too often it proves to be a hopeless journey of nostalgia, back to an idealized childhood and to intangibles that no longer exist.

Much is to be said for and against life alone in either a big city or a small town. Big cities offer privacy, good job opportunities, a chance to meet all kinds of people (especially men), and to enjoy music, theater, and art. Against which big cities can be lonely, dangerous, and very expensive. Small towns (or suburbia) can be cozy and comfortable. Distances are short, faces are familiar, the druggist, bank teller, grocer, etc., call you by name, community projects are easy to find, the cost of living is less, and you will need fewer clothes. Against which is the lack of privacy, dearth of men, a social life consisting almost exclusively of "couple people," and good jobs are scarce unless you have special qualifications.

Whatever you decide, don't burn all your bridges behind you. Keep in mind that this must be a trial period and that if it isn't successful, you can try something else.

There comes a time when you awaken one morning to the familiar awareness of loneliness and loss, followed by a sudden, overwhelming restlessness. The mail is cleaned up; you have come to terms with your finances; you have decided to sit tight in your present home for at least a year. Although friends and relatives continue to be attentive, dropping in from time to time, still you are seeing less and less of them.

Now, for perhaps the first time, you are facing a day with nothing whatever to do. Briefly you consider the chores that are lying in wait for you. The attic? Not yet. In your mind's eye you see the boxes of old clothes, love letters, scrapbooks, records. . . . No, you are not ready to clean up the attic. The front hall closet? Not a chance. It is still filled with his golf bags, fishing gear, skates . . . which must be given away. Even the freezer, crammed with last summer's bounty from the garden as well as many of his favorite desserts, is beyond you.

How long is it since you prepared a meal for guests? How long since your married daughter and her family dined at your house? Before your husband's death they came every Sunday, and it was a happy time of catching up on the week's news while the children played with their mother's toys, so carefully preserved for them. For a good many weeks your son-in-law has been picking you up each Sunday and driving you to their house for dinner.

It isn't easy, but you telephone your daughter and invite them all for Sunday dinner, overriding her startled protest of, "Mom, you come here—we love having you." You grab a pencil and pad—Sunday is day after tomorrow —and carefully write down your menu and marketing list. Roast beef and Yorkshire pudding for your son-in-law; spinach and mushroom soufflé for your daughter; and the ingredients for the upside-down chocolate cake that the children adore.

Since your market will deliver, you decide to walk. You stop in front of the five-and-ten to watch a mechanical duck dip its beak up and down in a trough of water, then dart into the store to buy surprise presents for the children.

The market is crowded but you move along quickly, filling your basket with such extravagant extras as fresh asparagus, a ripe avocado, and Bibb lettuce, as though seeing these delicacies for the first time. The flower stand catches your eye, and you buy a mad profusion of pink roses, lavender stock, and white baby's breath.

As you start walking briskly home you realize, with a joyous upsurge, that you are beginning your life over again. This is when you start marching, not tottering, into the future.

Chapter 3

YOU AND YOUR YOUNG CHILDREN

We, whose children are grown when death takes our husbands, comprise almost 90 percent of the widowed popu-
lation in this country. But the remaining 10 percent of us
are responsible for more than a million children, ranging
in ages from eighteen to young babies. Those of you in
this category must deal with a different set of problems.

First and most important—you are not alone. You are
sharing life with your family, but on an altogether different basis than before. Now you are totally responsible
for providing emotional and practical guidelines for your
children at a time when you could nicely use such help
yourself. And yet, being forced to think of those whom
you love and who are dependent upon you, can speed
your recovery.

I have talked to mothers of minors who have said, in
effect, "I don't know how I could have gone through this
without my children," as well as those who ask, "why do
people say children are such a blessing at a time like this?

For me they are only additional problems." Presumably both attitudes reflect feelings that antedated the tragedy.

At the time of sickness and death in a family small children are, of necessity, often overlooked. They are rushed off to grandma's or to a neighbor's; they are not allowed in the hospital; and though deeply aware of the confusion and tension surrounding them, they cannot understand it.

Eleanor D., fifty years after the event, is still angry whenever she recalls how her parents lured her and a younger brother (aged ten and eight, respectively) out of the house and shunted them off to a relative's home until after the funeral of their beloved baby sister. It was betrayal, as far as Eleanor was concerned, and never forgiven.

Death is rough on children—even young ones. I have known two five-year-olds who lost adored grandfathers. Andy, a bright, active little boy, used to eagerly look forward to his grandfather's daily visit in the late afternoon, on his way home from work. Together they played games, or Grandpa read aloud, with Andy curled up inside his arm. Suddenly Grandpa was gone, never to return. For weeks afterward Andy sat alone on the floor of his room every late afternoon, staring listlessly into space, and refusing to be diverted.

Jimmy, also blessed with a very special grandfather, seemed to take his death in stride but betrayed himself, from time to time, by silently brimming over with tears for no apparent reason. On his birthday, months later, his uncle, admiring the mountain of presents piled high on the breakfast table, said, "You're a lucky little boy,

Jimmy." "I am not," he answered sharply, "I lost my grand-father."

If this can be trauma, how much greater the agony when it concerns the death of a beloved father. Someone, preferably the mother if she possibly can, should break the news gently, honestly, and promptly. It is damaging to learn about this from outsiders. Explanations should be tailored to suit the age of the children, but must be explicit. It is so easy for a small child to feel rejected, overlooked, even to evolve the notion that he is somehow to blame. Had he been a better boy and not smashed his brand-new tricycle, mightn't Daddy . . . ?"

A psychiatrist, whom I questioned about this, wrote me saying, "A child's guilt may be based on actual anger he is feeling for his father at that particular time. Sometimes it may even be based on magic. Children often have hostile fantasies about their parents, and should one die, they are quite likely to think that the fantasy has had the magical effect of causing the death. Then, too, children may become disturbed at a parent's death, not only because of the grief and sense of loss they experience, but because they may feel it as a threat to their very existence. For example, the death of a father may raise in the child's mind the quite reasonable idea that the mother might also die, and then what will become of him?"

Carrying on as a single parent requires coming to grips with your own painful reality as fast as possible so that you can help your children with theirs. They, too, are suffering from shock and grief and need your sensitive understanding of how they are feeling. It is a crucial time in your relationship.

Eleven-year-old Elizabeth, an only child, was brought

home from summer camp to attend her father's funeral. His death, just before his fortieth birthday, came after a year of bedridden illness. During this entire time Elizabeth had been his loving slave, rushing home from school every afternoon to write his letters, read aloud, run errands, and do everything in her power to make him comfortable.

Reluctantly, at her mother's insistence, she had gone off to camp, hating to leave her father, and hoping against hope that some miracle would save him. Now that her worst fears had been realized, she begged to be allowed to stay home close to her mother—to comfort and be comforted. For a variety of reasons, none of them valid in the face of Elizabeth's anguish, her mother refused. And so, on the day after the funeral, regardless of her obvious revulsion at the idea of returning to camp life, she was shipped back. It created a rift between those two that has never healed.

There is no guide book to tell you what to do, how to answer questions, what attitude to take in any given situation connected with the death of your children's father. Your behavior will have to hinge on what kind of person you are, how aware, how you feel toward your children, and what your relationship with your husband had been.

Be your natural self. If they are old enough to understand, explain to your children that the cycle of every human being is birth, life, and death. Birth is a miracle, a joyous event. Once here, we tend to take life—living, growing, maturing—for granted, something that belongs to us. But death fills us with grief and fear. Grief for the loss of a loved one—so much the worse when he is young. Fear, because we identify ourselves with this bleak ex-

tinction. Since death is the inescapable fate of every human being, we should be taught to meet it with acceptance and faith. This is a tall order but, nevertheless, it helps if the matter is frankly discussed instead of nervously glossed over.

It does your children no harm to see you grieving—this is natural and right. A stiff upper lip may even suggest that you don't really care. I watched two boys, aged ten and twelve, in their own home immediately after their father's funeral service. With disbelief, akin to horror, they saw their bereaved mother offering drinks and passing trays of sandwiches to the assembled mourners, behaving, as far as her horrified sons were concerned, like a hostess at a cocktail party. They stood it as long as they could, but in a short time bolted from the room and the house. How much better if she had not made this preposterous effort but, instead, had been her natural, grieving self. Willing helpers would gladly have dispensed the hospitality, while the boys would then have stayed at her side, sharing the grief and the ordeal.

It is not possible for you to be a mother *and* a father, nor should you try. Some mothers feel that only by dedicating themselves to their children can they compensate for the loss of the father. "I live for my children," is perhaps another way of saying, "I live vicariously through my children," and is damaging for all concerned. For you, the mother, it means limiting your interests, your growth, and your social life at a time when you should be expanding all three. For your children, it imposes too much of a responsibility. Mother must be looked after, cared for.

Shortly after her husband's death, Janet C. overheard her three boys, aged twenty-two, nineteen, and seventeen, discussing arrangements for taking care of her. Jonathan, the oldest, had graduated from college and had both a job and a girl. Peter, the middle one, attended N.Y.U., and Robbie was still in high school.

"Let's work it out so that she's never alone at night," she heard Jonathan say. "We'll compare plans and schedules Sunday mornings and give priority to greasy grinds who have to work in the library." This last was aimed at Peter, well on his way toward a Junior Phi Beta Kappa key.

Two nights later, Janet told them her news.

"I've signed up for a night course in interior decorating," she told her astonished sons. "I'm going to try to get a job in that field, but first I need to know more about fabrics, color, design. The course is five nights a week, and Saturdays I'll be making 'field trips'—visiting different stores. I hope you won't feel neglected," she added, carefully ignoring the look of surprised relief flooding every face. She stuck it out for three long months before deciding that interior decorating was not for her. But it had served its purpose—by that time independent patterns had been established, and the boys felt free to live their own lives.

Share your grief, your thoughts, and your problems with your children, when feasible, but keep your identity intact. You are not just a mother, as circumstances seem to suggest. You are a person in your own right, and only by being yourself can you be of help to them. An outgoing mother with satisfying interests of her own, one who can combine discipline and guidance with love and understanding, must make a far better mother than a recluse, concentrating all her time and energy on her children.

As always, there are exceptions. Jeanette C., young, attractive, and happily married, was plunged into tragedy by the sudden death of her husband. After the initial shock and grief began to subside, she realistically faced her future. Finances were not a problem; but bringing up four children, ranging in age from eleven years to six months, by herself, posed all kinds of problems. What those children didn't need, in her judgment, was the insecurity or possible threat induced by their mother's social life, dating, and, perhaps, remarriage. What they *did* need, she decided, was her undivided attention. Four mature, happy, well-adjusted youngsters, successful in their careers and marriages, attest to the wisdom of her decision.

Don't idealize your husband to your children. This isn't to suggest that you should point out his shortcomings and faults. But someday you may again find happiness in marriage, and it will be easier for you and your children if another mate isn't being odiously compared to a paragon who, presumably, never existed.

Unless they are very small, give your children jobs to do, and let them know how much their help means to you. How could you get along without them! Eleven-year-old Johnny holds his nose and makes awful faces when he empties the garbage pail once a day (a job that's been his since his father's death three months ago), but he never forgets and wears a smug, man-of-the-house expression while he's doing it.

In another home sixteen-year-old Marianne has learned how to cook since her father's death forced her mother to find a job. She is fascinated and challenged by her new skill, and weekday evenings has a good dinner waiting for her mother and younger brother, Phil. After dinner Phil cleans up and does the dishes, and weekends their mother takes over, often providing simple party fare to which they are encouraged to invite their friends.

In most cases the death of the husband means reduced finances for his family. Here again, if your children are teen-agers or close, discuss the matter frankly with them. Given the facts concerning the family's needs, the financial status quo, the cost of living, and what you hope to accomplish by a full-time or part-time job, children tend to become cooperative partners. Such understanding on their part can be an incentive to get good grades, earn scholarships, work after school, save—all very much to the good.

Marjorie N., a working mother whose husband had died a few months earlier, listened to her four children, ranging in age from seventeen to eleven, enviously describing a new color television set that belonged to a cousin.

"It's beautiful," said Ritchie, the oldest. "It's got everything. Someday I'm going to own one."

"So am I," came a chorus from his sister and two younger brothers.

"What are we waiting for?" asked their mother, having just finished explaining their somewhat inelastic finances and how careful they must now be.

"Money," said Richard, and the others nodded agreement.

"Right," said their mother, "no other way of getting one. But I have an idea," she added. "I know that each of you needs every cent of allowance that you receive.

However, I'm willing to match every dollar that you can *earn* until we have enough to buy the television set. On one condition: Everyone must contribute something."

Everyone did. All four got busy in the neighborhood baby-sitting, delivering packages, walking dogs, shoveling snow, and in seven weeks the television set was installed. After this heady success, there was no stopping them. The following month four new savings accounts were opened in the local bank.

Don't feel that all your problems (and you will surely have them) stem from the fact that your husband isn't sharing them with you. Children are dropouts, run away from home, fail in school, join the drug circuit, get into all kinds of trouble in the most respectable, two-parent homes. About all that you can do is love your children and let them know it. It helps if you can find uncles, male cousins, or friends who will take an interest, especially in a growing boy who needs to relate to a member of his own sex. Someone to take him fishing, skiing, or to ball games—fun that he might have shared with his father.

In time you will have to face the problem of your own dating, and, for most of us, this is crucial. If you have done a good job of communicating and including your children in all phases of your life, you probably won't have much difficulty in explaining why dating is important for you and obtaining their approval and understanding.

Again, it all depends on you. If you begin dating madly as soon as possible in the frantic hope of finding another husband because you simply cannot face life without one, you may trigger all kinds of insecurity and fears in your children. Although the present situation may be anything but ideal, a stream of potential stepfathers (and don't think that your children won't consider them as such) can be anything from unsettling to terrifying.

On the other hand, if you explain to your children that you, as well as they, require a social life with your contemporaries which, of course, includes men, it makes very good sense. If, in time, you do become seriously involved and are considering a permanent relationship, talk it over with your children. If you cannot reach them, if they refuse to understand your feelings or cannot deal with their own hangups on the subject, seek professional help.

Watch out for sensitive areas. Lois T., tall, slim, and very beautiful, overheard Margot, her fat, adolescent daughter of seventeen, complaining to her best friend on the telephone.

"Mother has more dates than I do," she said bitterly. "It's just not fair."

It didn't take much soul-searching for Lois to realize that, absorbed in resolving her own problems, she had failed Margot. Now, for the first time, she really communicated with her daughter, describing her ruptured life, her loneliness, and what dates meant to her. Margot, treated as a confidante and not a rival, quickly regained her own perspective and, eventually, was able to accept and love her mother's new husband.

Married children can be counted on to encourage dating on the part of their mother. In fact, unless a legacy is threatened (this is dealt with in Chapter 10), most married sons and daughters are delighted when a mother finds happiness once again with a man.

But long before a happy ending can evolve, you will have been forced to make a series of major adjustments in terms of yourself, your children, and your social life. Since you are no longer half of a team, sharing with other couples such diverse activities as bowling, community fund-raising, bridge, anniversaries, New Year's Eve parties, country club dances, PTA, etc., your social life will take a different turn. You are now "an extra woman," "a fifth wheel," and how you handle this will affect your success as a single parent.

As previously suggested, you would do well to change your former social patterns, seek new people, new interests, new groups. Which brings me to Parents Without Partners, Inc.—an international organization started in the United States fifteen years ago that now has chapters all over the country, "dedicated to the interests and welfare of single parents and their children."

This organization is described in moving detail in a book called *Parents Without Partners* by Jim and Janet Egleson, published by E. P. Dutton & Company. Your public library can get you a copy.

Parents Without Partners, Inc. is a nonprofit, membership corporation offering its members a great variety of activities. It is designed to serve men and women, divorced or widowed, and group discussions are planned for each group separately. They deal with such questions as "How can a bereaved parent help himself shake a depressing and debilitating sense of loss?" "How can a mother deal with a child's troubled reaction to the loss of a father— withdrawal or anger?" "How does a parent's dating affect a teen-age child?" Guest speakers include doctors, lawyers, social workers, psychiatrists, and many others, who give lectures at scheduled meetings and welcome audience participation. Organized parent-child entertainment in-

cludes outings of all kinds—picnics, parties, visits to amuse-
ment parks, museums—all tailored to the age of the children involved, and designed "to give the single parent
and child a sense of 'family' good times in a congenial
group." Not least of their activities are the adult social
events planned to give single parents an opportunity of
meeting and knowing others in the same situation. The
membership in 1972 was eighty thousand and, according to George B. Williams, executive director, "has
doubled in size every third year of our existence."

Check it out for yourself. Write to:

> Parents Without Partners, Inc.
> 7910 Woodmont Avenue
> Washington, D.C. 20014

They will send you over-all information as well as help
you to contact your local chapter. This could bring you
new contacts, an interest shared with your children, and
the luxury of talking to people who know, firsthand, all
that you are going through and very much want to help.

Your children will look to you for a great deal. You
cannot be all things to them. But if you can give them
love and support, if you can help them to find their own
identities and worth without smothering or overprotect-
ing, if, above all else, you can look forward, not backward
—the chances are that your children will come through
handsomely.

Chapter 4

GETTING READY FOR ACTION

It would seem that barely have you solved one problem than another rears its head. For weeks you have been pushing this one aside, lacking the courage to tackle it, knowing only that, sooner or later, it must be met head on.

Now the time has come—the time when your out-of-town adult children no longer take turns visiting you, those living nearby must return to their own lives and responsibilities, and there is less and less coming and going on the part of your friends. Suddenly the impact of an empty house in which the silence screams is more than you can bear.

The problem boils down to whether you should live alone or try to find someone, on some basis or other, to share your life and your home.

Your mind casts about frantically for someone—anyone—who might be eligible. You think first of your bachelor brother, with whom you have great rapport. But he's a perennial party-giver, needs to have young people everlastingly around the house, and plays music from morning until night. You know that you couldn't take it.

There's Jennifer, your twenty-seven-year-old niece. You dearly love her but your mind boggles at the thought of taking on Jennifer and her disturbing emotional problems.

How about Charlotte, your college roommate? Her husband died a few years ago, and now she lives alone in the Midwest. You've always had an exceptionally good relationship with her and you know, for a fact, that she much prefers living in the East, loves the sea—everything you have to offer would appeal to her. But your interests are totally dissimilar, and it's been a long time since you've spent more than a few days together. If you're entirely honest, you'll admit that those few days were more than enough.

Then there's Evelyn, whose husband died about a year ago and who has been a lost soul ever since. You are old friends, congenial, share the same interests. Too dangerous. Evelyn is not only depressed, she is helpless and dependent. At this stage you are not ready to be a prop.

Still, you certainly want to find someone to live with. Look at all the advantages. It's very pleasant to have congenial company around the house—someone to share meals and responsibilities, weekends and holidays. Someone to unzip your dress, listen to your news, tell you when you've put on too much makeup. Someone with whom you can divide the chores, especially when entertaining, and certainly it is far cheaper when two share the expenses.

It sounds all plusses; but in fact it is nothing of the kind. A housemate to whom you can look for all this and more besides, is rare to the point of nonexistence. The hazards are enormous. Personality conflicts can develop like measles and spread over the entire relationship. The kitchen has yet to be invented that is large enough for two women, and no two ever seem able to agree on how to cook anything from a simple vegetable to an elaborate dessert. Financially you are apt to be on different levels, which means that one will be holding back while the other may feel pushed beyond her means.

Then, if one of you has a job, thus reducing the strain of too many hours together, sickness or retirement can change that. There is also the danger that friends will begin thinking of you as a pair and will continually invite you together, thus eliminating a good deal of social adventure.

Even a sister can backfire. Muriel B. happily agreed, soon after her husband's death, to sharing her home and all expenses with her widowed sister. They'd always gotten along beautifully in spite of a ten-year difference in their ages. In time fifty-three-year-old Muriel needed and wanted a new life, new friends, and, above all, male companionship. At the same time her sister turned into a cross between a mother and a chaperone. What had once been a fine relationship eroded beneath the pressure of criticism and endless compromise on whether to dine early or late, whether to eat in the kitchen or the dining room, whom to entertain and when. Eventually Muriel called a halt and the two separated. Superficially the wounds healed, but their good relationship was never entirely restored.

If you can possibly do so, avoid taking in family, for you will be risking an emotional holocaust. A sister can be difficult; a mother is usually worse. Madeleine G.

could never explain why she had thought having her
elderly mother move in soon after her husband's death
would be a good idea. True, they had always been close
and congenial, but from the vantage point of separate
homes and separate lives. Madeleine, now in her early
fifties, knew a mounting resentment as her mother began
bossing her around. It took the seemingly innocuous form
of, "That's your sixth cigarette since dinner, dear—I don't
think you realize how much you're smoking," or, "I'd
skip dessert for a while if I were you—you're beginning
to put on weight," and, too often, a plaintive, "I hope
you won't be awfully late getting home tonight; what
time *do* you expect to get home?" Eventually Madeleine
managed to find a job in another town. Awash with guilt
feelings and at fearful cost to their erstwhile good relationship, she managed to extricate herself from this impossible situation and move into a small apartment alone.

Sharing your home with someone who gets on your
nerves is endlessly abrasive. Especially if it is someone
set in her ways when those ways are diametrically op-
posed to yours. Someone who, charmingly but endlessly,
offers up small criticisms, the sum total of which can be
devastating. "If you're not careful, you are going to clog
the sink." "This coffee is too strong and really not good for
you." "If I were you I'd add a little Clorox to the water,"
ad infinitum. Since, to date, you've managed nicely without this superfluous advice, you'd like to continue doing
so. A trial run might uncover these and other irritations.

It can be done but, like everything else, it requires
careful planning, flexibility, a willingness to compromise
on all levels, and, above all, a clear-cut arrangement,

ahead of time, as to your freedom to come and go as you choose.

The greatest danger to you lies in moving in with married children. No matter how eagerly your daughter issues the invitation, nor how well you get along with your son-in-law, nor how much the grandchildren adore you: *Don't do it!* For it will be you, the mother and grandmother, who will make the adjustments. The generation gap is not a new invention. It has been in existence forever. You will risk losing your identity and being forced to live the life of the household in which you find yourself.

The complaints of widowed mothers living in the homes of married sons and daughters are endless. The grandchildren are noisy or inconsiderate; their care and feeding comes first; their wishes, preferences, and demands receive instant attention. Too little privacy, too many compromises, always the feeling that, in the true sense, this is not her home. Depending on whether she is included or excluded at dinner parties, she feels either superfluous or rejected.

Look back to the time when you and your husband were struggling with careers, children, and community projects. Back to the time when you were carving out your own enduring relationships with each other and your children—trying together to give those children everything you believed they needed most. Would you have wanted your widowed mother to move in with you, no matter how much you loved her?

From your son or daughter's point of view, you are an added problem where none is needed. Don't forget that they, too, have suffered trauma and loss through your husband's death and are deeply sensitive to your grief. But that doesn't make it any easier when you fail to see eye-to-eye on various matters. You'd be less than human if you didn't react to your fifteen-year-old grandson's refusal to bathe, change his underwear, or cut off at least a little of that shoulder-length hair. How can you manage to keep still when you discover, for a fact, what's going on between your seventeen-year-old granddaughter and the boy next door? But their parents have difficulty enough dealing with their children in today's world without criticism or interference from you.

Vacation time, intended for precious family junkets, poses problems, too. Should they invite you to come along, thus limiting their fun and freedom? Can they leave you home alone, thus risking hurt feelings on your part and guilt feelings on theirs?

The community activities, so absorbing to them and their contemporaries, will be crashing bores for you. You no longer feel passionately about PTA, Girl Scouts, or the problems of the school cafeteria. They, on the other hand, aren't madly interested in your work with senior citizens.

Like everything else, once in a while it works. Mrs. H. shared her married daughter's home with verve and charm for over twenty years when she died, just after her eighty-seventh birthday. From the very beginning both of them recognized the dangers inherent in such an arrangement and realistically took steps to avoid them. Mrs. H. occupied her own beautiful room, built as a wing on the second floor, that could be closed off for complete privacy. Here she grew magnificent gardenias, entertained her needle-work guild, and kept up her many interests and voluminous correspondence. No hurt feelings if she was not included in her daughter's and son-in-law's parties; instead she was served an appetizing and attractive meal on a tray in her room. No problem about transportation: When entirely convenient, she was driven by some member of the family; otherwise she traveled happily by bus. During her last years Christmas presents from her children always included a book of taxi tickets. Thus where resentment might have bloomed, instead there was understanding and appreciation on both sides. Rich dividends accrued from this arrangement—a grandmother in residence whom everyone adores can create a very special climate of love and security in a home.

But for every success story, there are thousands of failures. So assess your own situation carefully, weigh the pros and cons, and take your time. If you have a financial problem, the choice may not be yours. In that case you can only make the best of whatever solution presents itself.

Could you possibly live alone? It's not easy at first—discouraging, disheartening, and very lonely—but well worth fighting for.

The rewards are tremendous. You can do exactly as you please, eat what you like when you feel like it, smoke your head off, stay up for the late late show, take an afternoon nap. You are independent, can come and go as you choose, buy a dog, raise African violets, fill the house with kooky people. Above all else, you do not have to adjust to anyone's idiosyncrasies or peculiarities. If you have the courage to give it a try, you will probably succeed. Most of us do.

Assuming that you decide on a trial period of a few

months alone in your present home, this is the time to take action. Accept those invitations that friends continue to extend. Maybe you'd rather not, maybe a given party sounds too big or includes people who don't interest you. Maybe you just don't feel like making the effort, aren't ready to try your wings, would rather stay quietly at home.

Push yourself out! You've probably had a good many weeks, perhaps months, of convalescing and being pampered. It's possible that you are just the least bit spoiled. But the sooner you become part of the world around you, the sooner your total recovery.

Besides, you may be in for a surprise. It is just possible that the party you didn't want to attend will turn out to be a warm, friendly experience. Discovering that people are glad to see you and welcome your company is endearing proof that you are indeed a whole person— not the half that you had come to believe. Even if the party isn't the greatest, the news will be out that you are once again in circulation, and other invitations will follow. This, in turn, can lead to new friends, new relationships, and new experiences, at a time when you need them all.

One word of warning! This is a good time to develop a protective coat of armor. Here you are, returning to the social scene as an unattached woman. Until now you've taken your married status for granted. Suddenly you find yourself at a dinner party at which there are several married couples and one unattached man. You don't have to be a genius to figure out that he's been invited expressly for you, and you'd be blind not to notice how interested everyone is in your reactions to each other. You feel angry, humiliated, and a little foolish. It's been decades since you've made an effort to attract a man, and it's the last thing on earth you feel like doing now. Besides, you'd be less than human not to feel a little insulted. Compared to your husband . . .

Stop and think about it. The man involved is no fool either, and is probably just as uncomfortable as you. He also has landed in an awkward position. Your hosts haven't arranged this to be cruel—just the opposite. If you will make an effort to forget yourself, join the party, and make a contribution to the fun and conversation, the dividends, in terms of getting outside yourself and forgetting your troubles, can be enormous. The same holds true when you find yourself the only unattached woman with no extra man, or even one of several. Shades of the Kaufman-Ferber play, *Dinner at Eight,* in which a harried hostess, thanks to last-minute cancellations, is frantically trying to find extra men to balance the sexes at her dinner table. Finally her harassed husband is heard to mutter, "I thought we were inviting people for dining, not mating."

Having survived these various ordeals, now do some entertaining yourself. If cooking is your "thing," you have a beautiful headstart, second to none. If, in addition, you have a talent for assembling interesting, congenial people of assorted ages and professions, your invitations will be doubly welcome.

Be prepared for rough sledding the first few times you entertain. It's so easy to generate anxieties and fears. Do your guests really want to come, now that you are alone? Who will make the drinks—can you swing it by yourself? When the time comes you will discover that the men present always offer to help with the drinks, keep an eye out for refills, move chairs, and make themselves generally useful. It never fails.

You, too, will have the problem of extra women. In this country, according to the Bureau of Vital Statistics, unattached women outnumber unattached men by approximately 3½ to 1. Not only are more men than women struck down in their middle years by heart disease, stroke, and cancer, but wars and accidents take their toll, too. Added to this is the actuarial fact that the life expectancy of women above the age of fifty is six years longer than that of men.

However, even if women are in the majority, make sure that there are several men to balance. One or two men and hordes of women spell disaster. So try to find unattached males, any age, as long as they are attractive and fun. With those attributes they can't be either too young or too old.

Perhaps you always looked beautiful to your husband, but the rest of the world is going to be more critical. There is nothing comparable to an elegant beauty parlor for making a lady feel chic, desirable, and madly attractive. It can bolster sagging spirits, instill confidence, and is highly recommended before returning to the social scene. Beautiful clothes help, too. Your son may think that new dress madly extravagant, but you know better. You know what it's doing for you.

Prepare for the evenings when you are home alone, and make sure that there are not too many of them. Stack your bills in one pile, your unanswered letters in another, and make sure that you have plenty of new magazines and books on hand.

Use your telephone—it's a bargain in terms of what it can do for your morale. An extravagantly long conversation with a sister or close friend hundreds of miles away can lift a soggy evening to amazing heights. Call up nearby friends (not married ones—husbands take a dim view of evening conversations on their time) just to say "I've been thinking of you—how are you doing?" Everyone likes that kind of attention, and it often triggers spontaneous dates.

Keep in touch with married friends whom you value, even if you seem to be the one making the greater effort. "How's everything?" "Let's lunch." Only good can come of it.

Avoid the outsized pitfall that most women living alone tumble into—the danger of talking endlessly about yourself. It is born of a crying need for a sympathetic ear to listen to the trivia that you and your husband used to share. No one else will be interested in the endless details of how your car broke down at a busy intersection and all the trouble you had until a mechanic arrived. Nor will anyone be fascinated by the peculiarities or shortcomings of your cleaning woman unless they are excruciatingly funny.

It takes time to get used to living alone. It can be good or bad, interesting or dull, challenging or overwhelming. It all depends on you.

Chapter 5

SO YOU'RE GOING TO SHARE YOUR HOME?

If living alone is so frightening that you simply can't face it, or if you've experimented and found it impossible to adjust to an empty house, then by all means find someone to live with you. Assuming that you have no available friend or relative, look for tenants on one basis or another. This won't be difficult; in fact you'll find it astonishingly easy once you start looking around.

A word of warning: Take your time, move slowly—this is an important, far-reaching decision. Before committing yourself, decide on exactly what you wish to offer, what arrangements and conditions would be best for all concerned, what compromises you are willing to make.

Keep in mind when you are seeking tenants that your way of life may change because of a job, a romance, or any number of unforeseeable events. All good reasons for being careful and not making long-term commitments until you know exactly what you are doing.

Interview your prospects carefully. Find out as much as possible about their plans, intentions of staying in your city, interests, hobbies, and all else that might affect you. Although such an arrangement is not necessarily permanent, still, careful screening beforehand can save embarrassment and disappointment later.

Remember: This is a business deal and should be treated as such. No matter how informal the arrangement may be, draw up a lease containing everything that both you and your tenants agree to contribute to the household. What are you going to be responsible for in the way of repairs or redecorating? Can they sublet if they wish and, if so, are there any restrictions? Is the tenant responsible for the furnace, shoveling snow, or emptying garbage and trash cans? Check with the proper authorities before adding a second kitchen to your house. Last, but most important of all, before signing such a lease (even if it's only a friendly agreement involving no cash), check it out with your lawyer. Let him discover any omissions that may crop up at a later date and spell trouble. Helene M. has her lawyer to thank for a clause saying, "adults only." When her tenants of two years announced that they were expecting a baby, she helped them find attractive quarters elsewhere with no hard feelings.

There is a saying in New England, "Strong fences make good neighbors." If you and your tenants know your rights and bounds, spell it out, and leave nothing to chance, you are sure to have a successful relationship.

If you happen to live in a college town, get in touch with the university's personnel department. Through them you can probably find either a student, professor, or perhaps a student couple in need of a home. In almost any town you will find that grammar or high school teachers are possible tenants; so are couples living near Army or Navy bases.

Your Chamber of Commerce is another valuable resource for finding tenants. Tell your neighbors what you have in mind. The unlikeliest people sometimes produce exactly what you are seeking.

It can work beautifully. Margaret B., in Rochester, New York, consulted the university and, after carefully investigating, invited two foreign students (a young married couple from Iran) to share her home. Up to that time they had been living in a cheap, fourth-rate hotel, but even so, there were fast running out of funds. Margaret turned over her entire third floor (two bedrooms and a bathroom) to her guests and converted one of the bedrooms into a charming living-room study, complete with two desks and a television set. In addition, she agreed to provide their food.

In exchange they agreed to share the housework, thorough-clean on Saturdays, wash the car, shovel the sidewalks, and take care of other odd jobs. Whenever they all happened to be home at the same time, they drifted comfortably into the habit of dining together. When Margaret entertained, she included her tenants if she thought the party would be congenial—both for them and her guests. Occasionally they arranged to invite friends for dinner, and on those occasions Margaret elected either to dine out or have a tray in her room. For the young couple this arrangement spelled comfort, security, and, above all, an opportunity to complete their education. For Margaret the benefits were equally satisfactory. Her home was well looked after, she liked having someone in the house when she returned home alone late at night, and it was pleasant having congenial company at dinner. In addition, she could take off on trips with the comfortable knowledge that caretakers were in residence. Since, as a by-product, they achieved a warm, affectionate relationship, everyone profited by this arrangement.

Betsy L., a gay, attractive woman in her early fifties, with a talent for making the most of fortune and misfortune, tried living alone, after the death of her husband, and succeeded beautifully until her large, somewhat remote farmhouse was ransacked by hoodlums during her absence. The combination of loneliness and fear then drove her to seek tenants—but not until she had carefully drawn up a plan for sharing her home with strangers. Then, since she lived near a naval base, she made an appointment with the personnel director in charge of housing there.

"I'm probably looking for the impossible," she told him. "I'm seeking tenants, preferably a young couple, who are neat, considerate, and quiet. I know they won't be easy to find. However, if you can find such a pair, I'm ready to divide my house into three parts: your zone, my zone, and a demilitarized zone."

"Exactly what does that mean?" he asked, obviously amused.

"'Your zone' will belong to my tenants," she said, "and will consist of a large, comfortably furnished, combination living-dining room, a double bedroom, and bath. The 'demilitarized zone' will belong to all of us and includes the entrance hall (it's enormous and contains a huge fireplace), the kitchen, and the utility room, complete with washing machine, dryer, and a separate refrigerator for the exclusive use of my tenants. 'My zone' will be the rest of the house and will belong to me. Rent: one hundred dollars per month."

He found the ideal couple at once. The wife works as a supervisor for the telephone company; her husband is stationed at the base. They proved to be all that was expected of them, and more besides. While all hands agreed that they did not wish to share either housework or meals (each has the use of the kitchen at different hours), there is a pleasant relationship between them and an occasional exchange of such items as homemade bread or special desserts. At Christmas, the tenants, far from home and family, were included in Betsy's family dinner.

Jennifer T., in Cleveland, found a bright, young teacher whose husband was stationed overseas in the service and scheduled to remain away for two more years. This tenant shares the housework, pays a small rent, and comes and goes as she pleases. If both are home at the same time, they enjoy dining together and, since this happens only once or twice a week, they take turns entertaining each other. Both find the arrangement satisfactory.

This is not always the case. Annette C., soon after her husband's death, found a delightful young couple with a brand-new baby, who gave promise of being ideal tenants. Annette, then in her late forties and childless, was overjoyed at the prospect of having a baby in her home. She didn't stop to consider that tiny babies, who sleep around the clock in infancy, have a way of turning into noisy, destructive little boys who may even go a step farther and acquire a baby brother. It turned into a

disaster that was eventually resolved, but not before Annette had suffered through a good many harrowing mo-
ments. Finally this family of four was persuaded to move
into a home of its own.

Florence W. took on a charming couple who turned
out to be sloppy, irresponsible, and so careless of her belongings that she found herself in a constant state of
tension. Having committed herself, without reservation,
to sharing her home, dislodging them eventually proved
to be a job for her lawyer.

Soon after her husband's death, Peggy D. filled her
large house with college students and, for a short time,
reveled in being helpful, busy, and needed. The boys did
the chores, and the rent they paid solved her financial
problems. This idyllic arrangement bogged down when
she began to realize that, gradually, they had taken over
her entire house. Doors banged and voices could be
heard any hour of the day or night, too often welcoming
what appeared to be a steady stream of girls. Within a
few months she sold her house and moved into a small
apartment that offered peace and privacy.

Carol D. did a model job of finding tenants. She took
her time, interviewed applicants carefully, and learned
as much about them as she possibly could. Eventually
she found a young couple who qualified in every respect.
Since, in her case, they would be sharing part of the
house, she stipulated that she would like to hold monthly
meetings during the first year in order to review the situation and air grievances. Thus in an atmosphere of good-
will and consideration, they were able to iron out the
few difficulties that did crop up. That's a fine climate in
which to tackle anything.

Assuming that you have now resolved your problem of where and how to live, what are you going to do with yourself? You are still waking up each morning with no incentive to get up and face the day. Housework is negligible when you are not catering to the tastes and preferences of a man. When it comes to community projects, people are still tactfully refraining from intruding on your grief, and you are more than willing that this should be so. You've had your fill, for the time being at least, of those organizations you used to serve.

What it all adds up to is the unpleasant realization that you have nothing to do. As you cast about to remedy this, you take another big step forward.

Chapter 6

THE JOB HUNT

We come now to the question of jobs. If you need to support yourself, must be gainfully employed, you will have been fretting and fuming as to how soon you can get to work. The minute your grief begins to subside and you feel in control of yourself as well as your affairs, you will want to take action.

If you are on leave of absence from a job, so much the better. Get back as fast as you can. You will find understanding and help waiting for you at the office, and will discover that work can be a potent antidote to pain.

If you haven't been working since you got married and began raising a family but now need a job, must earn money to support yourself—did you once have a profession or skill? If so, try to find a refresher course in your own field. Times have changed, and so have techniques. If possible, track down some of the people with whom you once worked and who are still employed. Invite them for lunch or dinner away from the office—whatever is best for them. Tell them your problem, ask for help and advice. They will be able to tell you, in general, what the situation is, what changes have taken place. Chances are that they will welcome you back into the working world and do everything in their power to help.

Janet C. married and moved away from New York, where she had worked in sales promotion in the home furnishings field. Eighteen years later, after the sudden death of her husband, she moved back to New York and began looking for a much-needed job. Through the director of the Home Fashions League (of which she had once been a member), she learned that two trade shows—Notions and Linens—were in progress that very minute.

"Why don't you drop in and see what's going on?" the director suggested.

Timidly—eighteen years away from a job is a long time —she wandered aimlessly through the Notions show feeling removed, alien, and a little frightened. With nothing accomplished, she started for home but, appalled by her own cowardice, instead drove herself on to the Linen show. Again she drifted through the aisles, eager to leave and only half focusing on what was going on around her. Suddenly a display of plastic mats—the handsomest she had ever seen—caught her eye. Fired by her own enthusiasm, she began asking questions of the woman in charge of the booth and learned how quickly this product was catching on all over the country. To her own astonishment, she heard herself saying, "You have a beautiful line. I've had a good deal of experience in the home furnishings field, and I'd like to work for your firm. Are there any openings? Do you think there's a chance for me?" P.S.: She got the job.

Marjorie N. had been a legal secretary almost thirty years ago. Driven by acute need for income as well as for something to fill her now empty days (her husband had been very ill at home for over a year), she signed up for a refresher course in shorthand and typing as soon as she could pull herself together after his death. The very day she finished the school recommended her as secretary in the office of a brilliant, controversial judge where she was plunged into a fascinating new world in which there was little time to think of much other than the business at hand.

Jean D. had been a fund-raiser twenty-two years ago. It required very few weeks, with the help of a former co-worker, for her to span the years, learn new techniques, and find an excellent job.

If you've never before had a job but now must find one, get hold of a remarkable pamphlet entitled Job-Finding Techniques for Mature Women. It stems from the Women's Bureau, U. S. Department of Labor, and you have only to write to

> Superintendent of Documents
> U. S. Government Printing Office
> Washington, D.C. 20402

and enclose thirty cents, to obtain a copy.

In the Foreword of this pamphlet Elizabeth Duncan Koontz, Director of the Women's Bureau, states, "This pamphlet points out job-finding techniques available to mature women and is designed as a step-by-step guide to assist them to prepare for and find employment."

Its chapters include such vital information as,

> How to Do a Self-inventory
> How to Prepare a Résumé
> The Job Hunt

How to Prepare a Letter of Application
Guides to an Effective Interview
Training Opportunities

Don't let yourself be thrown by the fact that in today's society, youth is supposed to be at an all-time premium and, in some benighted circles, it is considered a miracle when an old lady of thirty can still totter around. We have figures to disprove this nonsense. According to Mary Dublin Keyserling, former director of the Women's Bureau of the U. S. Department of Labor, "Today the period in which we women are most likely to be employed is in our middle years, especially in the age bracket of forty-five to sixty-four." Since the grand total of women at work is approximately thirty-three million, you can see that there is hope for all of us. Here are some interesting figures:

Labor Force Participation of Middle-Aged and Older Women

August 1972*

Age	Number (in thousands)	Percent of Population (By age groups)
35–39	2,714	48.0
40–44	3,060	51.6
45–49	3,342	54.0
50–54	3,155	52.7
55–64	4,144	41.3
65 and over	1,079	9.3

Mrs. Koontz also has this to say: "Studies indicate that the mature worker is generally characterized by greater

*Source: *Employment and Earnings*, Vol. 19, No. 3, September 1972 (U. S. Department of Labor, Bureau of Labor Statistics).

stability on the job, less turnover, and with giving a very creditable performance."

Keep all these comforting facts in mind when some youngster in personnel gives you the impression that he thinks your best days are behind you. You may not be either young or beautiful, but you have some valuable compensations—such as maturity, good judgment, and a sense of responsibility. After all, presumably you have competently run your household, headed up all kinds of community projects, helped your husband (probably more than either of you realized), and now are ready to give your undivided attention to your job. Not so that cute, blond chick at the reception desk with an eye out for every passing male. You even have an edge on married women, who are known to be a calculated risk. Often they get pregnant, bored working, or find it unnecessary as their husbands climb up the executive ladder. Then, too, husbands may be shifted to other cities, as Vance Packard's *A Nation of Strangers* so conclusively proves. *You* have probably come to stay.

However, it isn't enough to bring only intangibles such as maturity or a cheerful disposition to a job. You will need some concrete skill such as typing, which is still a fine tool for prying open all kinds of doors. You can learn to type at night school in your local high, attend a secretarial school, or find a teacher, perhaps retired, who will give you private lessons at home. Fifty dollars or less will buy a good reconditioned office machine (much better for learning and practicing than a portable), and in addition to pounding out your homework, type everything you need to write, from personal letters to marketing lists. Speed comes quickly if you keep at it, and you will never starve if you are an accurate, careful typist. No matter how old or inexperienced you may be, somebody, somewhere, needs and wants you. If you've got brains besides, you're on the way up before you start.

Shorthand is something else again. Valuable to know, difficult to learn, less needed than formerly in today's world of dictaphones, copiers, and computers. Bide your time on that one until you know, for a fact, that your financial future will be enhanced by this skill.

Look at yourself through your potential employer's eyes. Does he see a well-groomed, attractively dressed applicant who looks interested, poised, and ready for work? Or is he uncomfortably aware of an overdressed gal, reeking of perfume, and nervously tugging at a short skirt that rides up the minute she sits down?

Wear simple, comfortable clothes and shoes—the best that you can afford. They will do wonders for your morale. Find clothes that won't need much upkeep, and for this, knits can't be beat. They are smart, warm, and durable. Make sure that your clothes don't call attention to any specific portion of your anatomy.

Be yourself. Be your own age, and remember that brightly dyed hair will add years to that age. Keep away from dangling earrings and fancy pins. Keep in mind that if you have something to offer, your employer isn't going to care how old you are. He probably won't hire you to model junior clothes, but that's the last thing you want to do, anyhow.

Listen carefully to what he has to say; talk as little as possible short of answering his questions. Never, *ever*, say, "I'll do *anything*." Nothing turns an employer off faster. Don't balk at a job that you think is beneath you.

Many a woman has risen to executive status by way of filing cabinets and reception desks. It doesn't take an employer long to discover talent that is being wasted in his office.

Carol G., totally untrained and badly spoiled by an extravagant, adoring husband, found herself, after twenty-seven years of marriage, looking for a paying job for the first time in her life. She learned typing, found a job in a life insurance office and, because she was smart and ambitious, spent her evenings learning the business. Today she is one of the most successful life underwriters in her agency.

Kathryn G., in her early fifties and mother of three married children, learned typing, then landed her first job in a typing pool in an advertising agency. There she discovered a hitherto unknown flair for words and today earns a comfortable living as a copywriter.

Eileen L., fragile (or so we thought), spoiled, and totally untrained for being anything but a grand lady, possessed one marketable asset: exquisite taste in interior decorating, which she had always beautifully demonstrated in her own home. Friends had been seeking her help and advice for years; suddenly, after her husband's death, it became known that she was in business. In the beginning, people engaged her services for small, redecorating jobs: a bedroom here, a dining room there. But as her reputation spread, jobs kept getting bigger and bigger. Now, at eighty-six, she is still in business, still highly successful. Those fragile ones can fool you.

Be sure to tell everyone you know that you are looking for a job. It is remarkable how often someone can fit you into a new venture. What you have been doing successfully as a volunteer can often be converted into a good-paying job. Eleanor J., a conscientious, hard-working fund-raiser for her local Community Chest, was grabbed by them the minute word got around that she was seeking a paying job. So, at fifty-eight, she became a professional for the first time in her life. Thanks to her volunteer experience, she brought special insights to her job, avoided the dangers and pitfalls inherent in working with women volunteers, and turned in a splendid performance.

Seek out the women you know who have good jobs. How did they get them? How much training was required? Is such training available? Study everything you can find concerning careers for women. You may be on the threshold of a fascinating, hitherto unknown field. Librarians can help you track down information, and I have yet to find one who doesn't become interested and involved in any project.

It's not always easy to hit your stride, but a lot depends on you. It may take time, a discouraging amount of time, to find a job, and when you do, at first it may not pay much nor be altogether to your liking. But once employed, you will be in a better position for either advancement or a change of jobs. Meanwhile, bring to the job as much loyalty, enthusiasm, and efficiency as you can muster. Forget your personal life, don't gripe, don't spread office gossip, don't try to be all things to all people (from mothering coworkers to "office wife"). Keep your mind on your work.

A job—almost any job—involves people, lunch hours, shared responsibility, joint efforts, crashing fatigue, success, disaster—all guaranteed to catapult you into the mainstream of the world around you and use up your energy as well. Weekends become a time for rest and relaxation, for enjoying the delicious luxury of reading, loafing, and entertaining, instead of empty, nightmare days and nights that serve only to underscore your loneliness.

Out of this welter of work experience, you will emerge a happier, more interesting person. Your life has definite purpose, you are busy, occupied—no time to waste on vain regrets, fancied slights, or what to do with the long, empty days. Friends will treasure their time with you, knowing how little you have to spare; and you, in turn, will become more selective. Instead of being a liability, you become an asset.

Perhaps you have skills, hobbies, or special interests that don't fit into the conventional world of business. Make them work for you. Are you a fantastic cook, a gifted gardener, a knowledgeable gal about antiques? Have you a flair for demonstrating? Does real estate fascinate you? Have you had special experience with pets? Can you teach bridge? What do you most enjoy doing? Whatever it is, it could pyramid into a career. Pepperidge Farm bread started in a lady's kitchen. What's going on in yours?

Look around you and see what's lacking in your community, then figure out a way to supply that need. Marguerite E., widowed and alone at fifty-nine, with no special training or skill and a pressing need to earn money, learned how to operate a travel agency, then induced her bank to open a travel department (there was none in her town) and to put her in charge at no salary until she proved what she could do. It soon became apparent that she could do a great deal, thanks to a large clientele stemming from local organizations in which she had served. Not only did this turn into a profitable job, but it carried with it such fringe benefits as trips to foreign countries at no cost. Thus a new and fascinating world opened up for her.

Marjorie J., a lady of taste and style, started at scratch with no know-how at all. She masterminded weddings, from the bride's trousseau down to the last white peppermint, and received a percentage from everyone with whom she did business along the way. This, in turn, led to other affairs, such as office parties, ceremonial dinners, political receptions, and anniversary celebrations. Since she was clever and imaginative, no two functions were ever alike, and she was profitably in demand from one end of the year to the other.

Irene B. plans gardens and, with the help of a talented young Italian, executes her beautiful "legends." She has a small, choice nursery containing stock that is unusual and very much in demand.

Are you a skilled photographer? Linda B., living in greatly reduced circumstances after her husband's death, managed to put three boys through college with the help of her trusty camera. She tracks down subjects everywhere: new babies in the hospital, "before and after" houses, weddings, family celebrations, children in the park, newly decorated rooms—the possibilities are endless. *Everyone* wants pictures.

Do you like selling? For the most part, jobs in this field require a minimum of training and can usually be found close to home which saves time and transportation costs. Make sure that you really like the products you are expected to sell. When enthusiasm is genuine, it's contagious.

Before taking any job, examine carefully what is required of you physically. How many hours will you be on your feet? Can you work well under pressure? Will it be necessary? Have you the stamina for an eight-hour day? Be very careful not to take on more than you can comfortably handle. The price of fatigue and discouragement is exorbitant.

In answer to an inquiry of mine, Mrs. Koontz of the U. S. Department of Labor wrote, "The fields which seem to be the most receptive to mature women returning to the labor force after an absence are: clerical work, retail trades, and health service occupations. There are more training opportunities in health services because of acute shortage of workers. Many vocational-technical high schools now provide training opportunities for adults, especially in clerical work."

Are you an outstanding shopper? Do you understand values, know how to buy the best for the least money? Comparison shoppers are very much in demand, and you can easily be trained for such a job.

Perhaps you need to find work that provides housing. Look for a job as housemother in a school, college, or institution. Some hotel jobs furnish accommodations; so do jobs on shipboard or in country clubs. Perhaps you'd enjoy being a companion for an elderly lady, especially one with a passion for travel.

Unless you have the hide of a rhinoceros and the stamina of an ox, avoid door-to-door selling. It's tough, guaranteed to diminish your confidence, can prove dangerous, and is exhausting and frustrating. It can also be very lucrative—especially in the field of cosmetics—but you will earn every cent you make.

Selling from home—magazine subscriptions, Christmas cards, stationery, paper guest towels and napkins—is neither easy nor profitable. It takes a lot of time telephoning and delivering orders to make a respectable income, and you must realize that customers may be moved more by pity than need, which will be demoralizing for you. Friends can buy only so much; then the going gets really tough. Use it as a last resort, and make sure that everything you carry is unusual and attractive.

Don't get involved in a job requiring a cash outlay on your part for special training, equipment, uniforms, or transportation (meaning the necessity of supplying your own car). Such jobs are suspect.

Unless you have had a great deal of experience, going into business for yourself is risky. Most of us cherish the notion that we could successfully operate our own little gift shop, restaurant, or bookstore. Most of these small ventures get swallowed up, one way or another, and disappear.

Avoid night work that brings you home late. Not only can it be dangerous, but it makes for an off-balance way of life at a time when you need to be part of the social scene.

There is always a market for homemade products, provided they are uniquely good. The possibilities are endless: homemade bread, pies, pizzas, quiches, trays of hors d'oeuvres, patchwork quilts, fancy dish towels, aprons, toys, jams, jellies, pickles, and dozens more. Barbara E. supported herself entirely from the sale of expensive, delicious, altogether wonderful chocolate caramels. They were so good that they became practically a status symbol in her hometown. Aline G. sold *schnecken*—a glorified honeybun—and couldn't keep up with her orders. Eleanor M. designed elegant smocks—so lovely that they made one feel glamorous even when standing over a hot stove. Enough women paid twenty-five dollars apiece for her to live more than comfortably on the proceeds.

As with everything else, you will find advantages and disadvantages to working from home. On the plus side, the costs are at a minimum, attractive tax deductions are permissible if you use part of your house for your business, and it is less strenuous than a full-time outside job. Against which you are at the mercy of your customers, who will not hesitate to call you at any hour of the day or night; your friends will not respect your working hours (you're at home, aren't you, so why can't you talk on the telephone?); and you, yourself, will succumb to the temptation of stopping long enough to whip up a dessert and start the pot roast. While you're at it, you might as well toss the laundry into the washing machine and fill the dishwasher.

Perhaps you need to augment your income but don't require a full-time job. There are dozens of possibilities: part-time salesladies, typists, answering service, baby-sitters, proofreaders, file clerks, etc. In today's working world there are 7½ million women working thirty-four hours or less a week. Of course, pay and fringe benefits are scaled down along with the hours, but that is to be expected.

If you can't find a part-time job that suits you, invent

one. Mildred T., with talent for interior decorating, discovered a fascinating shop displaying, higgledy-piggledy, merchandise that she found beautiful and unusual. Observing that the shop was always jammed with frustrated customers, she offered her services free, on a trial basis, for four hours a day. Within a very short time order replaced chaos, merchandise could be quickly located, and Mildred was firmly entrenched at a handsome salary.

Beatrice L., living in a summer resort, specialized in basket beach lunches. During the late spring, summer, and early fall, she averaged slightly more than 50 baskets a day at $2.25 apiece. Costs low, profits high. Just what she needed to augment her income.

Lillian B. organized a baby-sitting pool in which the mothers pay for each other's services in kind. Thus whenever one of them engages a baby-sitter for a specified number of hours, she then owes the pool an equal number of baby-sitting hours. It works exactly like drawing blood from a bloodbank, and fathers are eligible to help reduce the debt. Lillian operates her unique employment bureau mornings only, from nine to twelve (except for emergency calls). For her services she receives a monthly fee of fifteen dollars from each mother. Thus the families involved have the advantage of hiring responsible, adult baby-sitters at almost no cost, and while Lillian hasn't exactly gotten rich from this venture, she does make a small, steady income and has the satisfaction of being a boon to the young couples in her community.

Don't expect a job—any job—to be endlessly fascinating. Inevitably there will be a certain amount of monotonous routine, repetition, and boredom in any kind of work. There will also be fulfillment, exhilaration, and satisfaction. The need to earn money can be a blessing because it will take you out of yourself and help bring your world back into focus. Once again you belong.

Chapter 7

CONTINUING EDUCATION

Perhaps you don't need to be gainfully employed, or at least not for the time being. What you do need is an absorbing, vital interest to take up the slack of your days and give purpose to your life. It won't be difficult to find. In fact, everyone is looking for you—that is, if you are a reliable, hard-working, conscientious volunteer. Such a one is indeed a pearl beyond price.

Here, too, skill at typing makes you especially valuable. Political organizations (very exciting if you are truly involved, and they're teeming with men), hospitals, Community Chests, NAACP, Care, Sane, Thrift Shops, day care centers—all these and more besides need help.

Perhaps you prefer working directly with people. Some of us can survive only if we know that someone, somewhere, needs us. In that case you might choose to be a volunteer in an agency serving people, such as the blind, the ill, the elderly, or the handicapped.

Do you have a way with children? If so, and you are between the ages of sixty and ninety-three, are in a low-income category, and are physically fit, you might like to investigate the Foster Grandparent Program.

Write to

Action
Office of Economic Opportunity
Washington, D.C. 20525

for a brochure supplying all details. This is a remarkably effective program, both in terms of the children and the foster grandparents. It fulfills vital needs of both. Its stated main purpose is to give love and care to children.

Foster grandparents serve only in institutions and agencies as part of a child-care team. Before qualifying, each grandparent must have forty hours of orientation in the specific work he or she is appointed to do. The program calls for four hours per day, five days a week, and each grandparent ministers to two children during that time. Foster grandparents receive what is called a "stipend" of $1,670 a year—the maximum that the law allows without diminishing Social Security payments, unless the recipient is over seventy-two. From that age on, Social Security payments are not affected by earnings, no matter how large they may be. In addition, foster grandparents are reimbursed for transportation costs, served one meal each working day, and are given a complete physical examination at the beginning of every year.

Plenty of volunteer jobs require no training at all, but there is a limit to what such volunteers will be permitted to do. Since volunteers are not always punctual, dependable, hard-working characters, organizations tend to reserve their most routine, least challenging jobs for them until they prove their worth. In fact, volunteers are seldom taken seriously unless they treat their work as though they were professionals. "Come on in and we'll find something for you to do," is the classic response to volunteers offering their services.

Knowing how to give physical therapy, help a retarded child, organize a senior citizens club, translate books into Braille, etc., require special knowledge. The new term "paraprofessional" means someone trained to give supportive help to a professional on a far more advanced level than that of an untrained volunteer. Such training can be obtained in social service agencies, hospitals, and home services. Investigate the resources of your community to find out what it has to offer in the way of special training that might interest you. If you can't find what you want, check nearby towns. Once you start investigating, you are sure to find a project or service that appeals to you and in which you can competently serve.

Perhaps you've always wanted to go back to school, prepare yourself for an interesting job. Adults in classes today number an estimated twenty-five million. They can be found finishing high school or college, getting a masters degree, learning anything and everything: typing; shorthand; selling; cooking; office management; training to be a travel agent, a dietician, a marriage counselor, an investment counselor—there is no end to the list. If you can afford a year or two without a job, eventually you will get a better-paying one as the result of education and training.

Don't be afraid to go back to school, and don't let friends or relatives discourage you. They will list the difficulties: "Wait until you see how much quicker and smarter the youngsters are." "Have you stopped to think that there won't be anyone around in your age group?" "What do you need to go through all this for, anyway?"

Pay no attention. If you want more education, go after it. Your government is again interested in helping. Send $1.10 to that wonderful

Superintendent of Documents
U. S. Government Printing Office
Washington, D.C. 20402

and ask for Pamphlet No. 10, *Continuing Education Programs for Women.* It lists approximately 450 programs, by states, and is designed to "help make it possible for women to engage in activities that use their individual abilities and energies." You may find something just around the corner from where you live that offers a challenging experience and a lifelong interest.

This booklet, also under the aegis of Mrs. Koontz of the Women's Bureau of the U. S. Department of Labor, covers the following:

New Action for New Needs
Reasons Behind the Return to College
Rising Job Interest of Adult Women
Educational Services Requested
Examples of Educational Programs
Special Degree Programs for Adults
Value of Continuing Education Programs

Appendixes

A. Schools with Special Programs or
Services for Adult Women by States

B. Related Services or Programs for
Adult Women by States

C. Guide to Selected Features of
Programs and Services Reported

D. Federal Funds for Continuing Education
Programs

E. Questions for Program Planners

F. Selected Readings

If you live in or near Boston and qualify, you can obtain a challenging booklet entitled *The Next Step* (a guide to part-time opportunities in Greater Boston for the educated women) by sending $1.50 to

The Radcliffe Institute for Independent Study
78 Mount Auburn Street
Cambridge, Mass. 02138

Its Table of Contents offers

Choosing the Next Step: An Introduction
Educational Opportunities
Colleges and Universities: Degree Programs
Continuing Education for Adults
Special Training Opportunities

Opportunities for Volunteers
Possibilities for the Volunteer
Planning a Volunteer Career
Voluntary Associations in Greater Boston

Employment Opportunities
Mature Women as Potential Employees
Résumés and Interviews
Counseling Facilities and Sources of Information
Employment Agencies
Samples of Part-time Jobs

Beware of tempting advertisements urging you to take home study courses. Many of them are phonies—expensive and worthless. Some are excellent. You might begin by consulting your local school on the subject and find out which ones it endorses. At the same time, write to

Accrediting Commission of the National Home Study Council
1601 18th Street, N.W.
Washington, D.C. 20009

asking for a list of privately owned home study agencies whose standards they approve. Also write to

National School of Home Study
229 Park Avenue South
New York, N.Y. 10038

asking for their brochure of home study courses. You may find something on their list that wouldn't have occurred to you but has great appeal.

Probably the best-known accredited schools offering courses that will give you a high school diploma or an equivalency certificate are

Lasalle Extension University
417 South Dearborn
Chicago, Ill. 60605

International Correspondence School
Scranton, Pa. 18501

National School of Home Study
229 Park Avenue South
New York, N.Y. 10038

and there are many more. Once you start sleuthing, you will discover much more than is listed here. This is intended only to point you in the right direction.

However, go slowly. Find out if you are equipped to handle the difficulties and discipline of working alone at home and getting your homework off on time. It can be discouraging, and this may not be the right moment for you to take on a solitary assignment. If you feel sure that you can do it, start out with a trial spin of one course. You will quickly find out if this is right for you, and you can then go on to a more extensive program.

If you have a high school degree but want special training that will qualify you for a specific job, inquire of someone in the field as to how you can obtain the necessary training. It is easy to get information at the source as to how to proceed.

Home courses in the arts—notably writing—have proved only too often to be a con game, and you will wind up a gullible target if you're not careful. If you happen to be an amusing raconteur or write an exceptionally good letter, friends have probably been telling you for years that you ought to write a book or short stories, ought to use that lovely talent professionally. Stuff that isn't nearly as good as yours gets published every day in the week.

You've been planning on doing something about this, sometime, someday, and now along comes an advertisement that is irresistible. A national organization, headed, so they say, by well-known, prominent writers (whose names you recognize) who have banded together for the altruistic purpose of helping unknown writers achieve fame, success, and money. You send them a fat check and, for a short time, manuscripts travel back and forth from you to, presumably, one or another of those eminent authors. Such is not the case. A few years ago a top-flight national magazine published an exposé of perhaps the largest and best-known of the writing schools. It proved conclusively that canned criticisms were parceled out to credulous writers by a flock of trained housewives (trained in the art of guessing which critique best suited the manuscript in hand) and that the "eminent authors" earned their outsized paychecks solely from the use of their names. The number of dropouts is tremendous, and so is the profit—but not for you.

Agents who offer to read manuscripts for a fee are also suspect. If your work is first-rate, an agent will be happy to represent you for a standard percentage of your royalties. If you have talent for writing, painting, sculpting— any of the arts—you won't need to be goaded into action by seductive advertisements. It will be difficult to stop you.

Now is the time for you to discover what you most want to do and learn how to do it. You are no longer affected by your husband's job, his commitments, or his preferences. Take your time, investigate carefully, then go after whatever appeals most. You are now in a position to change your life style, make new contacts, move, even to train for work in a foreign country. It is entirely up to you.

Perhaps you are eligible for a grant, or at least a stipend from one source or another. Women over thirty-five are being encouraged to obtain training and go back to work. Look around . . . talk to all kinds of people . . . ask questions. Sooner or later you will find what you are seeking.

Maybe, for the time being, you'd like to try something brand new but less ambitious than the suggestions offered in this chapter. If you live near a good adult education center (there are classes both day and night in some of them), you will find a fascinating variety of subjects to choose from: law for the layman, Spanish, flower arranging, investments and the stock market, painting, sewing, writing, macrame, cooking, upholstering, bookbinding, furniture restoring . . . the list is endless, and you can choose what you like. So sign up and get to work.

"Work" is the magic word. It can be your life raft, your incentive to move ahead. As you hurry off to work—paid, volunteer, or pursuing a hobby—you will know the exhilaration of belonging to the world around you.

Chapter 8

DOS, DON'TS, AND BOOBY TRAPS

Under rough, tough circumstances, it helps to know what to expect, what to avoid, what to tackle. This is especially true as you brace yourself over and over again to getting along without your husband. Looking back, you realize how much you accepted, took for granted, and now desperately miss.

Don't let yourself wallow in self-pity. It can engulf you like a tidal wave and be just as damaging. It is a luxury that you cannot afford. Don't keep talking about your grief, your loss, the marvelous times you and your husband used to have. No one wants to hear about how much he liked chicken livers, never touched coffee, enjoyed a nightcap before he went to bed. A certain lady cannot play bridge without constantly explaining how she would have bid a difficult hand had she been playing with Joe. Since Joe has been dead for more than two years, this does nothing to brighten the evening for anybody.

You do not have a monopoly on grief. In one way or

another, more or less, sooner or later, everyone has a
share. How you deal with yours can spell the difference
between alienating people or obtaining their warm sympathy and understanding.

Look around you, lady. There are thousands, millions
like you, but not all of them have as much to be grateful
for. Count your blessings at the top of your lungs. What
have you got to be thankful for? Do you have devoted
children, loyal and loving friends and relatives, freedom
from financial worry, resources within yourself, cherished
memories? Many have only a fraction of these blessings to
go on with.

While you're at it, count your husband's blessings too.
Did he live to see a beloved son graduate from college or
a daughter marching happily down the aisle? Did he enjoy his work, have fun with his grandchildren, travel to
exciting and lovely places?

How to be a widow is how to be a person. Discover
your identity—not as a widow, but as *you*. Reinforce
what you are, who you are. The act of marriage splits
people in two, turns them into half a couple. Now you
are no longer Mrs. Doctor, Mrs. Lawyer—you are Mary
Anne Smith, not a half but a whole person, standing on
your own two feet, with an obligation to yourself to be
as interesting, as informed, and as attractive as you can
possibly be.

Widowhood is neither a state of grace nor disgrace—
it is a fact of life. The popular image of a successful
widow is someone who doesn't make you uncomfortable.
But it should be more than that. Rather it should be
someone who moves forward—growing, developing, reaching out for life instead of backing away.

There are camouflaged booby traps that can trip you along the way. Watch out for married couples. All unwittingly, they can annihilate you. If they are too devoted, they emphasize your loss. If hostile to each other, you cannot bear to see the waste.

Don't drop in on a married friend around the time her husband returns from work. You won't like what it does to you. Don't stay late in the evening if you are a couple's only guest for dinner. Nothing is more irritating than a woman who stays and stays and *stays* (even if she's the best company on earth), unless it's the one who talks and talks and *talks* (never having mastered the art of listening). Your audience will be sympathetic up to a point, reminding themselves over and over again that poor You have no one to go home to, no one with whom to talk. But it will be a long time before they expose themselves to *that* again.

"Couple people" can be warm and wonderful, or they can unintentionally throw mean curves. The former are patient and undemanding, ready to include you and give you the benefit of every doubt. They realize that recovery can be slow and unpredictable and are helpfully at hand when you need them.

The latter don't quite know how to handle you and your misery. They expect you to pull yourself together in record time and meanwhile find dealing with you awkward. Will you dampen a dinner party with your grief? Will you throw it off-balance by being an extra woman, and a troubled one at that? So they say, "Call on me for anything at any time," thus salving their consciences when they omit you from social gatherings. They told you they'd come to your rescue whenever you needed them, didn't they?

Or the phone will ring and you will recognize the voice of a good friend.

"Johnny has a business dinner meeting tonight," she may say. "Come on over and have dinner with me."

What you would really have liked is to have been included in that fabulous dinner party they gave last week and about which everyone is still raving. It is infuriating to know that had your husband been alive, you would surely have been included. Second best would be an invitation when Johnny is home. Cozy little dinners with ladies whose husbands are out for the evening have lost their charm. So you say "Yes" or "No" depending on circumstances or your mood of the moment, but either way you are deeply resentful. If you can generate a little tolerance and understanding, you won't mind so much. Sure, she lacks sensitivity but she, herself, hasn't experienced your suffering and probably does value you and your friendship. She didn't have to invite you at all, did she?

Old friends who at first look out for you, include you, try to help in every possible way, cannot be expected to do this indefinitely. There will come a dinner party when they can't find an extra man and don't want a lopsided table. So, for this once, they'll skip you. Maybe it happens again—after which they begin to feel guilty and uncomfortable where you are concerned. Again, remember that it's not personal. It doesn't mean that they preferred your husband to you. It means only that you pose problems, and not entirely because you are single, unattached, but because you are now independent, responsible to no one, free to come and go as you please at a time when you are probably emotionally unstable. Even your best friend doesn't intend to give you an opportunity of weeping on *her* husband's shoulder.

So, as time goes on and you begin to feel like a whole person, your own person, resist the temptation to cling to the old crowd. Try to get involved with new and different groups. Search for them in church, in local organizations, in volunteer work, at bridge duplicates, fund-raising drives, or travel tours. Get out of that closed, protective circle of family and friends; widen your horizons. These new friends will love you for yourself alone. In addition, they will not be identified with memories of other times.

Be on your guard for special calender dates, such as your husband's birthday or your wedding anniversary. Don't be a sitting target, a helpless victim of memory and nostalgia. Make plans. Invite guests to dine in an elegant restaurant or to see an absorbing movie or play. Preferably guests to whom this will be a treat.

Watch out for unexpected blows; go on the assumption that no one really wants to hurt you even if, sometimes, it taxes your credulity—such as the moment when you open a letter from your husband's class at college inviting you to be their guest at an important reunion. You will look with disbelief at the salutation, "Dear Widow."

Be ready for insensitive, tactless remarks, and don't let them demolish you—such as one stemming from an unusually intelligent woman addressing herself to three widows, all of whom had lost their husbands less than three year before. The hostess had included the lady because her husband was away for the night on a business trip.

"Johnny and I are going on a tour of Italy and France,"

she told her captive audience. "You may be very sure that I've checked with the tour director to make certain that the group isn't swarming with unattached women."

A startled silence followed this amazing confidence; then Margot, the youngest and most recently widowed of the three, said quietly and with immense dignity, "We don't *choose* to be 'unattached women.' It's a dreadful thing that has happened to us."

In your quest for yourself, for new contacts, new experiences, you will do foolish things as well as sensible ones. Maybe you'll join an Arthur Murray dance group. You've always been a good dancer, it's healthy exercise, and it will fill a lot of empty hours. Besides, you'll be in the arms of an attractive young man, a wonderful dancer, who will teach you intricate new steps, and the physical exercise will give you a sense of relief and well-being. You begin to look forward to those hours, go more often, buy bigger and bigger blocks of tickets. Long before they are used up, you phase out. You have had enough, recognize it for what it is: an ersatz stopgap that no longer serves its purpose. You wish that you hadn't been quite so foolishly extravagant (tickets cannot be redeemed), but you chalk it up to experience. You have learned again the valuable lesson of *no long-term commitments*.

Don't demand attention from your family; be grateful when it comes your way. Remember what fun it used to be to visit an elderly aunt who never said, "Where have you been all this time?" in a voice implicit with reproach? Instead she marveled at how pretty you looked, listened with rapt attention to your most trivial news, always produced delectable refreshments. When it came time to leave, she never, ever, said, "Oh dear, are you going *already?*"

Don't be dependent on your children! It's easy to demand too much, expect too much, make an everlasting nuisance of yourself. Don't call your son at the office unless it's a dire emergency. He can wait until he gets home to learn that you've overdrawn your bank account or nicked your car on a hydrant parking downtown. You can handle these and similar crises all by yourself. Don't call your busy daughter to ask, "What's new?" She's probably racing through chores to get out, and predictably she will generate resentment. Let them seek you out, and when they do, make sure that they never suffer needless guilt feelings at your hands. They love you, but they're busy people and haven't as much free time as you do.

Reciprocate. On every level with everybody. It is the keystone of successful living. Do more than your share, do it oftener than need be, participate, give. Try to think about others; you may be very sure that they, in turn, will look out for you. It's a natural by-product. Conversely, "I do so wish that I could repay your wonderful hospitality, but being all alone . . ." are famous last words. Women seldom get a chance to utter them twice.

You are now the head of your household. If you don't already know, learn the answers to a lot of simple questions, such as where your husband bought liquor, and where he took the car to be greased and oiled. How often do you need to buy stickers, tires; and what else should you know about your car? As you run out of gas for the first time in your life, you will learn, the hard way, that it is now your eye that must check the gauge. To whom do you turn with an insurance problem? Do you have a safe deposit box, and if so, does someone, other than yourself, know where the key can be found? If you need new and expensive appliances, how do you judge which is the best buy? What is the name and number of your plumber, electrician? Make a list of everything and everyone vital to your welfare, and be sure to include the police and fire departments.

Each of us knows a remarkable person who has met tragedy with bravery and gallantry. My candidate for this very special hall of fame is Elizabeth L., whose attractive and adored husband died at the age of fifty-two, shortly before her own fiftieth birthday and at a time when all four of their children had grown up and left home for marriage or college.

Soon after his death, Elizabeth moved out of their enormous bedroom, with its king-sized double bed, into a small, adjoining study—but not until the room had been whitewashed and three of its walls filled with happy family pictures taken on the beach, sailing before the wind, during cross-country junkets of all kinds. One entire wall—the wall of the future—she left bare, ready and waiting for whatever the future held in store.

At Christmastime, a few months after her husband's death, all the children, two with spouses and small babies, came home to spend the holidays with her. Her four-line Christmas card, sent to friends all over the country, tells the story of Elizabeth:

> FRIENDS IN JOY AND FRIENDS IN SORROW
> WHO HELPED ME FACE THE GREAT TOMORROW
> MAY GOD BLESS EACH ONE SO DEAR
> WHO MEANT SO MUCH TO ME THIS YEAR

Somehow she managed to be the one to offer comfort.

Chapter 9

TRIPS AND TRIPPING

Sooner or later a restless, floundering You will suddenly yearn to go away. Although you have made remarkable adjustments, better than you ever believed possible, still, the need to get away from it all, even for a short time, is overpowering.

Nostalgically you recall the fun that you and your husband used to have planning trips, reading aloud to each other from brochures and travel books. It was he who took care of passports and visas, traveler's checks and reservations, inoculations and vaccinations.

Now, though you can think of little else, you lack the courage to take off. It wouldn't be any fun without him, and there is no one to take his place.

But long years of travel holidays have infused you with a wanderlust you didn't know you had. You must get away, must shake off, for a time at least, the small pinpricks of pain that still plague your days. You know that you are infinitely better. As a newly reformed smoker eventually reaches the stage where, for hours at a time, he doesn't think of cigarettes, so you have reached the stage where, for hours at a time, you are unmindful of sorrow.

You make up your mind to go away. Another cross-road has been reached; so has another problem. Your children are involved in their own lives, possibly all of them are married, responsible for the well-being of spouses and children. Even if they were free to go with you, it wouldn't be ideal, for them nor for you. The generation gap is not a figment of the imagination but a very real chasm that stretches between you and your children. It can be bridged by love and understanding, which doesn't necessarily mean that you can be successful traveling companions.

Cousin Alice is a possibility, but she hates walking—something you very much enjoy doing, especially in new and foreign places. There's Margot, a college classmate, with whom you've maintained a close friendship throughout the years, but it's a standing joke that she goes to Europe (or any other place) for the sole purpose of shopping, and you hate shopping. Besides, let's face it. Do you really want to eat three meals a day with either of them?

Nevertheless, and in spite of known hazards, the chances are that for the first trip after your husband's death, you will find someone to accompany you. Even though you may be living alone successfully, you are doing it in familiar surroundings. It takes a different kind of courage to board a ship or plane by yourself.

No matter: your first trip will be another step in the right direction and will signal the welcome news that you are continuing to forge ahead. However, it will help immensely if you and your companion agree, beforehand, to go your separate ways when the spirit moves you, with no hurt feelings. You may wish to look up old friends by yourself, do some special shopping, leisurely browse through a bookstore at your own tempo. If she sleeps late mornings and you are an early riser, let it be understood that you will meet her someplace for lunch. If one of you is invited by a man to dinner, let it be agreed that this will supersede any previous plans for being together. Finances should be frankly discussed as to how much each can afford for accommodations, entertaining, and entertainment.

Go in a spirit of fun and adventure. Make an effort not to dampen each other's spirits with reminiscences of happy bygone trips. Compromise whenever possible. One may want a cocktail at the bar every night; the other prefers her drink at the dinner table. One doesn't care much for music; the other is indifferent to art galleries. One isn't much interested in food; the other is a gourmet always ready for an adventure in eating. So everybody does a little of everything.

Don't let anyone talk you into a threesome. Three ladies traveling together are doomed. Sooner or later they bog down into two against one—a situation guaranteed to fracture friendships and spoil the trip for at least two.

There are decided advantages to traveling with someone, especially if you're lucky enough to have an old friend available—someone whose company you've always enjoyed. It is much cheaper when two share a hotel bedroom, you are seldom alone, and, if your tastes are similar, it's more fun to hear a concert, see a play, shop, sightsee, or dine with a good companion. The catch is that you never know what you're getting into until you try it and, by that time, it may be too late to remedy the situation.

Helene and Marcia, congenial friends living at opposite ends of the country, both widowed and alone, happily took off for a holiday in Mexico. It had been years since they'd been together—long enough for Helene to have forgotten Marcia's congenital inability to be on time. For anything, anywhere. Whether they arranged to meet in a museum, a restaurant, or at a bus stop, Marcia arrived late. Very late. A small thing like this can have a cumulative, abrasive effect. In the end Helene, outraged at the sum total of all the waiting, cut the trip short and flew home. Their friendship was also cut short.

When it comes time to take off for your second trip, stop to think. All over the world pairs of middle-aged to elderly ladies are traveling together, eating meals, sightseeing, sipping afternoon tea—a cozy little entity that no one would dream of disturbing. No one needs to look after them, invite them to join a party, talk to them, or pay any attention to them whatever. They have each other, don't they? Certainly a man will think twice before inviting *two* ladies to join him for a drink or dinner.

Everyone takes care of the lady traveling alone. Everyone talks to her: men, women, children, and couples. People who will forever ignore ladies in pairs are sensitively aware of the lady alone.

This is not to suggest that you travel by yourself when making brief stays. Certainly a hotel room in London, Paris, Rome, or any large city where you have no friends or contacts, can be a chilly, lonely experience, no matter how fascinating the sightseeing. For this you need Cousin Alice.

A "special interest" tour can be a splendid compromise between traveling with a companion or traveling alone. You can select the one that appeals most to you from a very long list. Tours vary: long or short, bargain or luxury, large groups or small, with accent on anything from gourmet food, wine-tasting, music, theater, art, history, or anthropology to skiing, golf, tennis, and more besides. Consult a travel bureau on what's available in your sphere of interest.

The advantages are many. Accommodations, transportation, and the handling of baggage will be no problem of yours. You don't even need to understand the foreign money nor speak the language of the countries you are visiting. You will have plenty of companionship without spending too much of your time with any one person. You won't need to take the initiative—your days and nights will be crammed with sightseeing and entertainment.

In case I've convinced you that tours are all plusses, they're not. Often they are too strenuous (even if you skip some of the offerings). You are always on the move, and there is seldom enough time to get acquainted with a place before you are on your way to the next stop. And before you are through, you may very well become tired of traveling in mass formation and seeing, day in and day out, the too familiar faces of your tour companions.

Sooner or later you are going to begin speculating as to whether or not you could handle a trip by yourself.

It takes courage the first time, lots of it, just like anything else. But you've probably listened to glowing reports from adventurous friends and are wondering whether or not you have the guts to try it. There's only one way to find out.

I practiced what I now preach. For my first trip, I traveled with a close, lifetime friend whose eccentricities and peculiarities I knew as well as her virtues and charms, and she knew mine. We divided a three-week junket between Rome and London. Because of her familiarity with both the city and the language, she was our "cruise director" in Italy and, for the same reasons, I was in charge in London. We tangled just once, and it was I who flunked. On the night we reached London, I insisted that she dine with me and a friend she didn't care for. She, resourceful and at home in any country, objected. I wouldn't take "No" for an answer. End result: just what I deserved. You won't be so foolish.

For my second trip (and the first alone), I carefully assessed the possibilities and picked Mexico—a country I'd never visited and hence would not be battling nostalgic memories. Since I had plenty of time, wished to learn the language, and do some writing, I booked myself into the Instituto at San Miguel de Allende and signed up for Spanish and their Writers' Workshop.

The trip from Mexico City to San Miguel will be forever engraved in my head. For some reason I couldn't get a ticket for the first-class bus; to this day I don't know what class bus I was on. What I do know is that it contained crates of fruits and vegetables (not in prime condition), some goats and chickens ditto, a couple of dogs, a pig or two, quite a few crying babies, lots of garlic, and me.

We arrived in the market place on a Saturday night, and on that evening Mexicans in the market place are drunken Mexicans. They looked fierce (they're not), and my Spanish evaporated as I clutched my bags and monotonously repeated "taxi, taxi," which turned out to be an international word, and a little boy brought me one. Even little Mexican boys look out for ladies traveling alone.

Arrived at my hotel, I hated everything in sight, including the guests and dinner. By bedtime I'd had enough of Mexico and decided not to unpack, to spend Sunday visiting churches and sightseeing, and to leave early Monday morning.

On Monday morning I had it out with myself. If after, say, a week in San Miguel, I still loathed it, I would be entitled to quit. What I wasn't entitled to was chickening out so fast. Not if I wished to keep a remnant of my self-respect. With which I unpacked, registered at the Instituto, and behaved as though there to stay.

It didn't take anything like a week for me to discover that I was having the time of my life. There we were—white and black, Jew and Gentile, Mexican and American —all ages, all sizes, happily "doing our thing." I have never been afraid of going anyplace alone since. As a matter of fact, I never am alone, and neither will you be if you will go out to meet your fate.

Isn't there someplace that you've always wanted to visit? Now's your chance. Start a project for yourself. Find out everything you can about the country, the peo-

ple, climate, culture, and industries as well as the tiny,
unusual inns along the way. Accumulate as much knowledge as you can—then *go!* Whether by air, land, or sea,
whether first-class or tourist, freighter or luxury liner—
go!

When you reach your destination, stay awhile, at least
long enough to absorb the flavor, learn the customs, and
study the language. If possible, take your holiday in the
off-season, when no reservations are needed and when
you can be flexible instead of jumping from reservation
to reservation.

Talk to everyone, even if you have just a smattering of
their language. Whether you are in the market place, on
the piazza, sitting in buses or parks—people will be interested in you because you're a friendly foreigner.

By staying in small inns you will find it easy to strike
up friendships along the way. Don't sit back and wait to
be discovered. Use any old ploy to make contact: How
nice it is to hear English spoken, where are you from,
where have you been traveling? It's just possible that the
attractive, middle-aged couple sitting in the lounge have
been globe-trotting alone for quite a while and will welcome your company. When you tell them that you've
heard raves about an unusual native place where you
hear the food is excellent and, besides, it's inexpensive
and clean, they might think it a great idea if you all
dined there together. Of course you'll make it clear that
you will go only on condition that you may pay your
own way.

If you love the sea, enjoy all kinds of people, are fascinated by new places and don't have to live either by the

clock or a fixed schedule—you are a natural for freighter travel. Write to:

> Harian Publications
> 1000 Prince Street
> Greenlawn, N.Y. 11740

> and

> Traveltips
> 40–21 Bell Boulevard
> Bayside, N.Y. 11361

They will supply you with masses of useful information as to itineraries, approximate length of time involved, cost of trips, and outstanding buys, as well as information on rules and regulations, countries and ports of embarcation, and all else that you might like to know.

Freighter trips can be a real adventure, according to the people I have been able to interview, but you must bring along some unique, built-in qualities for the long, quiet days at sea when your main diversion will be reading and talking. If you don't have resources within yourself, you will be restless and unhappy. Passengers on freighters are usually middle-aged to elderly couples, teachers on sabbatical, early retirees. Age span? From early fifties to the seventies, although there are occasionally exceptions at both ends. The ships call at interesting ports, do not stick to schedules, and do not guarantee how long or short a stay will be made in any given port. It all depends on cargo, which has priority over any other consideration. Hence there is no certainty as to the length of the journey—it hinges entirely on the acquisition and disposal of cargo along the way. Crews are care-

fully selected—it is part of their job to provide a pleasant,
interesting voyage for the passengers. The food is usually
simple but good, designed primarily to please the cap-
tain's palate.

Avoid cruises—they can be disasters for unattached
women. Not always, of course; you may be lucky, you
may be an exception, but it's risky. Passengers average
approximately fifty women, twenty married couples, and
ten men. These last form a tiny, powerful minority. The
competition is killing and cutting. Who are these men
who think that such a trip would be fun? Their reasons
for being aboard are suspect, and so are they. The married couples, for the most part, seek each other out, unable or unwilling to look out for the masses of unattached
women aboard. Don't be one of them.

Resorts are also danger zones, filled with hopeful females, predatory females, and always a dearth of men.
Again the competition is fierce, the rewards small.

Once you have decided on the itinerary of a trip,
accumulate as many names of friends of friends along
the way as you possibly can. Any strange or foreign place
is enhanced a thousand times by finding a welcoming face,
even if it belongs to a stranger. Let's assume that you are
going to London and have been given the names of half
a dozen people to look up. The minute you arrive, mail
each a note (written before you left home, if possible)
explaining who you are, mentioning the name of the mutual friend, and inviting them for lunch or to have drinks
with you, depending on whether you are addressing a
couple, a lady, or an unattached man. Don't telephone—
this can throw your listener off-balance, and you risk embarrassment for both of you. Most of the women I know

report that this method sparks telephone calls, notes, flowers, and invitations from hostesses who have been given time to consider what they'd like to do about entertaining you.

There are a few hard-and-fast rules that apply when you are traveling alone. When invited to join a group for a day's outing or sightseeing, be meticulous about paying your own way. Since this can be clumsy, corner one of the men in the party and ask him to be your banker, then reimburse him at the end of the day. If, as part of a small group, you have been invited to several parties, give an elegant one of your own. Even if your guests protest, assure you that it isn't necessary, go right ahead and do it. It's easy to make excuses for yourself, rationalize, back out of hosting a party. It's also easy to find yourself on the outside looking in. Plan your party carefully, make it as lavish as you can afford. If it's a meal, arrange to pay in advance and adjust up or down the next day. Watching a woman fumble with a check, compute the tip, and pick up change can be awkward and embarrassing. But if dinner is delicious and no money appears to change hands, there is nothing to do but enjoy it.

You are returning from your first trip alone—sunburned, relaxed, happy to be back, full of amusing stories about your adventures. You'd be blind not to notice how relieved and happy your children are that it all went off so well. They've worried a bit, not at all sure that you could make it alone. But all they ever say is, "You're quite a gal, Mom."

Chapter 10

THE MEN IN YOUR LIFE

If you haven't already done so, you are going to discover that it's a man's world. Nowhere is this more apparent than widow versus widower.

The latter, apart from his grief, hasn't a social problem in the world. He is at a premium: cosseted, pampered, sought after, deluged with invitations. Women drop like ninepins all around him—he can pick and choose, decide what he wants and grab it. He belongs to another branch of the powerful minority.

A widow, on the other hand, falls into one of three categories. She is either a menace, a drag, or a woman struggling to gain a foothold in a world that once belonged to her.

She's a menace if she's young and beautiful, and that means anything under forty-five. Wives worry, husbands run the gamut from fascinated interest to eager passes, and no matter how removed in heart she may be, she will find herself at the center of the storm.

She's a drag if she's older and sorry for herself. If she

believes that she's the only woman in the world to know
such sorrow, such suffering; if she talks endlessly about
herself and her tragedy to anyone who will listen; if she
continually brings her husband's name into the conversation with tears and reminiscences—she's an outsized
drag.

The majority of us belong to the third category. Since
most men are older than their wives and die sooner, the
average age for beginning life alone is somewhere in the
fifties. But the fifties, or even the sixties, are vulnerable
ages for women, especially for those who have enjoyed
male thinking, male companionship, male love.

Inevitably the day will dawn when you begin to wonder
if you will ever love or be loved again. Have you anything
left to give, anything worth having? Are you attractive
enough to interest a man—the kind of man who appeals
to you? Running parallel with these thoughts and yearn-
ings comes a devastating sense of disloyalty and faith-
lessness. If you loved your husband so much, how can you
be fantasying his replacement?

Because you're human, that's why. It helps to know
that practically everyone feels exactly as you do. Most of
us want a man of our own—to love and be loved by, to
need us, to share our lives. We want him so badly that,
too often, judgment is suspended and common sense van-
ishes. We grasp at straws.

Let's assume that you are middle-aged, attractive,
lonely, and trying desperately to start your life over again.
You will probably make a great many mistakes as the new
You drifts back into a thorny world.

You are surprised when the husband of a good friend
telephones one afternoon and, after inquiring solicitously

THE MEN IN YOUR LIFE

about your health and welfare, suggests dropping in for a drink on his way home. You are touched and pleased, and welcome him warmly with a hug and a kiss. It feels so *good* to have a man's arms around you for a few seconds.

A few days later he appears again—this time without warning and his cheerful, "just passing through on my way home and thought I'd find out how you're getting along," lifts your spirits sky high. It so happens that you need some advice about a few matters, and he is delighted to be of help.

You begin to look forward to his visits and count yourself lucky in having such a good friend. Afterward you find it difficult to rationalize your own stupidity. How could you be so surprised, so caught off-balance, when your "friend" made his intentions clear? It seems that he and Lisa don't get along in bed, and haven't for a long time. It means nothing to either of them. He's every bit as lonely as you and has always had a special feeling for you.

Here's where you stop to think. It's all so logical, so plausible. Under these circumstances, whom would you be hurting? What will it mean if you *do* go to bed with him? Will it provide physical release, will it lead to a continuing good and friendly relationship? Or will it mean a cheapening of yourself in a sham relationship? Will you be swamped by guilt feelings, hate yourself for your gullibility? Will you end up losing Lisa's valued friendship?

No one can answer these questions for you, and you'll have difficulty answering them for yourself. Vulnerable, bewildered, tempted, insecure, you—depending on circumstances—will probably settle for trial and error with different men at different times and for different reasons. In so doing you will learn a great deal about yourself as well as the men in your life.

This is a time for caution, for carefully assessing the relationships that come your way. Is this man looking for a quick, unimportant affair, is he using your defenselessness to satisfy or work out his own needs? Or does he really care?

Beware of philanderers. You are fair game, now, but to you it is not a game. It is a haven—but one that can backfire and prove dreadfully damaging. This is not the time for you to be made to feel inadequate, unattractive, nor have to ask yourself, "Why couldn't I hold him?" You won't have the good sense to know that no one could hold *that* one.

Inevitably this is a time of confusion and uncertainty, and you will have to struggle through it. How differentiate between affection and opportunism? How recognize blatant flattery when you long to believe that it's genuine admiration? You, so vulnerable and lonely for male companionship, are more than ready to accept everything at face value. You want to believe that you are beautiful and desirable. Who doesn't? Even though, deep down, you may harbor a sneaking suspicion that there might be an ulterior motive to your swain's extravagant compliments.

Listen to that ugly little warning. Even though it hurts, ask yourself a few searching questions. Could he possibly be leading up to a loan, an investment, to marriage for the wrong reasons? As long as you face these possibilities you are safe instead of being a helpless, defenseless target for exploitation—that is, if in addition and before taking any permanent action, you consult the legal member of your new team and have your swain checked out. Not only can you save yourself heartache and loss of self-respect, you may also save your economic future.

Sally J., an attractive mother of grown children, had been cared for and protected by an adoring husband for twenty-seven years. About a year after her husband's death, she fell deeply in love with a newcomer to her community. They were continually together and, after a brief affair, he asked her to marry him. Bliss—once again life was beautiful.

A short time before the wedding he mentioned a fabulous business proposition in which he had been offered a share but, unfortunately, didn't have enough fluid capital to take advantage of the opportunity. Sally, unused to business decisions of any kind and totally committed to her fiancé, without consulting anyone turned over the necessary thirty-five thousand dollars, a sizable proportion of her husband's estate. A few days later he vanished. Looking back, she was forced to admit that she'd been a prize fool. In her joy at being loved again, she had accepted everything on faith, ignoring much that should have been of interest and importance in a man whose life she planned to share. Now she was faced not only with shattered emotions, but also with sharply reduced finances.

So be careful. Sharpen your judgment, be a bit skeptical at first; but not so suspicious that you don't recognize fine friendship and a warm and wonderful relationship without any strings when it comes your way.

Stop and think hard before embarking on an affair with a married man. There are tempting advantages. Someone to cook for, to fuss over, to feed your drooping ego. A reason for dressing up, for looking your best—he can provide much that you have been missing. He can also provide frustration, jealousy, and discontent such as you never dreamed possible.

You cannot be seen together in public; holidays and weekends belong to his family; there will be times when you cannot even reach him by telephone, no matter how great your need. It will be you who make the adjustments and compromises, you who play a waiting game, listening for the telephone to ring, meanwhile asking yourself a few pertinent, if unpleasant, questions: such as exactly how committed he is to this family he claims to scorn; do he and Mary really occupy separate bedrooms, go their separate ways? If true, why isn't he getting a divorce? It's difficult to believe that he's only waiting until Junior gets through college or Mary Jane gets married. Since your relationship is static, you worry about the slow atrophy of your romance and find yourself longing for a respectable, conventional, married life, the kind that you and your husband had and that you see all around you. Why doesn't he want this as much as you? . . . If he really loves you, why doesn't he . . . ? Eventually you face the unpleasant fact that your real problem is whether or not you can get along without him. Finally you realize that the chances of your ever coming first are slim. Can you settle for half a loaf?

If the answer is "Yes," build up a life apart from him. It should include consuming work, interesting friends, a varied social life. You can't always be on tap. Otherwise the relationship is doomed.

You may find that much younger men drift into your

life. They may be seeking a port of call, good food, drinks, amusing conversation, or company for an occasional movie or show. Sometimes they will come in pairs and welcome you into their deviate world, where you not only pose no threat, but can be an important, happy adjunct to their lives. They give as much as they take, or more. Whether singly or in pairs, these can be important, satisfying relationships.

How do you feel about a second marriage? For some, no matter what the circumstances, it is stark necessity. Regardless of such considerations as mutual interests, tastes, backgrounds, or financial security, these frantic women plunge into a second marriage believing that there is no satisfactory way of life without a mate. A quick replacement, born of desperation, can create worse problems than loneliness. Too often friends are responsible, doing everything in their power to bring about a remarriage. An unattached woman can be a problem in many ways, and what could be nicer than if good old Joe and Marge got married? Possibly lots of things could be nicer. Joe has a nasty temper, he's not awfully well, and they haven't much in common. But Marge, pushed by friends and blinded by her own needs, starts life over again with Joe.

Some women discover and appreciate the advantages of living alone. This is not to say that their grief is less, nor that they do not continue mourning in their hearts. But they have accepted the inevitable and, after months or years of independence, freedom of all kinds, they may balk at starting over again with all the necessary adjustments and compromises. What are your new love's food idiosyncrasies? Is he neat or sloppy, does he smoke in bed, hate having a light on when he's ready for sleep?

Does he leave the bathroom a wet shambles after shower-ing? Is he chronically late for appointments? For some of us, who have tasted the heady freedom of living exactly as we choose, there is little temptation to start over again in marriage. For some of us, there is no other way of life.

A successful marriage depends not only on mutual at-traction and interests, but also on what went before. Did you have a good marriage, including a happy sex relation-ship? Did he? Or are you trying to compensate for what you feel that you may have missed? Are you looking for lost youth, or are you ready for a mature, happy, com-mitted relationship?

The temptation to remarry can be overwhelming. If you've done it successfully once, why can't you do it again? You can. But first make doubly sure that the man in your life measures up to your standards and that you are marrying each other for the right reasons: Old-fash-ioned reasons like love, respect, admiration, and a long-ing to share. Take your time, even though you aren't young. You may have forgotten that marriage is for breakfasts, for Sundays, for keeps.

Your chances are good. Given two mature people, gen-uinely in love, they have some decided advantages. No need to cope with the tensions and struggles of young marriage; time to relax and enjoy each other without worrying about jobs or climbing elusive ladders; less fa-tigue, more leisure, longer holidays, and, above all else, a deep awareness of old mistakes and the determination not to repeat them.

Before marrying for the second time, a couple would be well to visit a lawyer and together learn all that there is to know about "antenuptial agreements." Unlike Wills (which are unilateral and can be changed at any time for any reason), such agreements are bilateral and irrevocable.

The ramifications are endless. Perhaps the lady will be giving up pensions, Social Security, or trust funds inherited from her husband and without which she would have a financial struggle, should she find herself alone again. Perhaps her husband-to-be will want to compensate her for such losses, depending, of course, on her circumstances and his own. Perhaps she is the richer of the two, and wishes to make sure that her new husband is comfortable if he outlives her. Very possibly both are financially secure and agree to eliminate each other entirely from their respective estates.

Antenuptial agreements, skillfully handled, remove all doubts and fears on the part of the offspring involved as to why their respective parents are marrying each other. Both her children and his have a stake in the estates involved, and family relationships can be strengthened when an inheritance is not in jeopardy. Often trust agreements are formed, with the children of the deceased eventually acquiring all the capital.

The variety of antenuptial agreements are many, and your lawyer will help you to work out the one best suited to your needs. It is proof of faith, trust, and love when such an agreement is drawn, and it's a good idea to inform all the children involved as to what is taking place.

The second marriage can be as happy as the first. It will be different, bring other satisfactions and rewards. But if you are intelligent and lucky *and* marry for the right reasons, the second "he" can share and brighten the rest of your life.

POSTSCRIPT

For each of us there is a different ending, depending, in part, on how we have met the biggest challenge of our lives. One and all, we have had to learn that we can no longer ride to glory on our husbands' coattails, nor on anything else, for that matter, except our own two feet.

Assuming that you have met this challenge head on— whatever you're doing, wherever you are—you are your own woman, able to handle your life. Whether you are living alone successfully or have found a job that turns you on, whether you have happily remarried or embarked on a new profession, you are not only finding your wings, but the whole, new You is in orbit.